AS SACRED TO US

AS SACRED TO US

Simon Pokagon's Birch Bark Stories in Their Contexts

Edited by Blaire Morseau

MICHIGAN STATE UNIVERSITY PRESS | *East Lansing*

♾ The paper used in this publication meets the minimum requirements of
ANSI/NISO Z39.48-1992 (R 1997) (Permanence of Paper).

Michigan State University Press
East Lansing, Michigan 48823-5245

Printed and bound in the United States of America.

Library of Congress Cataloging-in-Publication Data
Names: Morseau, Blaire, editor.
Title: As sacred to us : Simon Pokagon's birch bark stories in their contexts / edited by Blaire Morseau.
Other titles: American Indian studies series.
Description: East Lansing : Michigan State University Press, 2023. |
Series: American Indian studies series | Includes bibliographical references.
Identifiers: LCCN 2023001819 | ISBN 9781611864625 (paperback) | ISBN 9781609177362 | ISBN 9781628955026
Subjects: LCSH: Pokagon, Simon, 1830–1899—Criticism and interpretation. | Potawatomi literature—Michigan—History and
criticism. | American literature—Indian authors—History and criticism.
Classification: LCC E99.P8 P64 2023 | DDC 897/.31609—dc23/eng/20230201
LC record available at https://lccn.loc.gov/2023001819

Cover design by Erin Kirk
Cover art Kelly Church Birch Bark Biting Bumblebees

Visit Michigan State University Press at www.msupress.org

Contents

Preface

This collection assembles recent discoveries and new interpretations from community members, Potawatomi-language speakers, and scholars with regard to a collection of thinly peeled and elegantly bound nineteenth-century birch bark books by Simon Pokagon. While an unknown number of these birch bark books are accessioned in museums and archives around the country, the specific texts from which this volume is written are housed at the Archives of the Pokagon Band of Potawatomi located in Dowagiac, Michigan. The stories were originally published by Pokagon's attorney, C. H. Engle, between 1893 and 1901. The content of the stories printed on the small rectangular pages of white birch—four titles in total—are transcribed in full here and framed by contributors who are experts in history, Native literary traditions, Potawatomi and other Algonquian languages, and even the geology of places in Michigan for which the stories are localized.

Pokagon's nineteenth-century birch bark books have been used in college classes for decades so that students could engage with Native stories, nineteenth-century settler colonial resistance narratives, and the history of anthropology, just to name a few. But now these birch bark stories are contextualized with new insights into the science of Indigenous oral history, the politics of Native representation, and the multiple layers of significance woven into the Potawatomi language. The wide-ranging interdisciplinary interests in Pokagon's birch bark books are evidenced by this unique collection of scholarly and community insights about his work. As such, this book is not narrowly defined by academic assessments or scholarly interventions divorced from community perspectives, but rather are framed by the expertise of both professional researchers and Indigenous traditional knowledge holders. Consistency in style and reader accessibility is balanced in this work with the value of scholarly and community-based Potawatomi language, culture, and history so that this is a text that is valuable to community members in addition to scholarly researchers.

Pokagon's use of Indigenous languages in this text are referenced as *Anishinaabemowin*, but sometimes referred to as *Bodwéwadmimwen*. While not mutually exclusive, they are similar. Anishinaabemowin is the more generalized Ojibwe spelling to describe the language or dialects spoken by the Potawatomi, Odawa, and Ojibwe peoples, while Bodwéwadmimwen is specific to Potawatomi peoples' language. In what has been grouped into the Algonquian language family in North America by linguists and anthropologists, Pokagon blends distinctly Ojibwe words and phrases that do not exist in the Potawatomi linguistic vernacular with, at times, romanticized translations into English. For this reason, as well as for clarity and consistency, the larger umbrella term "Anishinaabemowin" or "the Anishinaabe language" is used more often than Bodwéwadmimwen or the Potawatomi language. As advanced Potawatomi language specialist Bmejwen Kyle Malott explains:

> Pokagon sometimes uses words that cannot be found in Potawatomi, Odawa or Ojibwe. Phrases such as *How-waw-tuck* translated by Pokagon as "The Almighty" in *Pottawatamie Book of Genesis* could possibly be attributed to the Mascouten people who he references as the tribe that was in the southwest Michigan area before the Potawatomi. Similarly, there are instances of what seems to be Anishinaabe words awkwardly plugged into places of the English sentence in ways that don't work for Anishinaabemowin. There are several possibilities for this, one of which might be that an editor took notes on Pokagon's stories but

didn't have knowledge of how the Potawatomi or related languages are structured grammatically.[1]

Similarly noted in the 2011 republication of Pokagon's novel *Queen of the Woods*, Pokagon's awkward use of Potawatomi language in a predominantly English-language text "could be because Simon's father, Leopold, was Ojibwe and Odawa, because contemporary writers he knew were Ojibwe and Odawa, or because his editors made changes to conform to their own notions of standards of the time."[2] These literary techniques, combined with over a century of orthographic change in the Potawatomi language community, presented peculiar challenges to the birch bark books' republication in *As Sacred to Us*. Updating the spelling of the Potawatomi language used by Pokagon to the contemporary spelling system adopted by the Pokagon Band of Potawatomi Language Program—now called the Pokagon Ėthë Bodwéwadmimwat Department—was considered by the contributors and the editor. It was determined, however, that there is value to language learners and historians to see how Pokagon oscillates between different language communities in his narrative style. Erasing his intentional use of phrasing (assuming it was his and not an editor's decision) to adhere to twenty-first-century standards would efface Pokagon's versification and idiomatic expressions. His original translations into English are kept; however, they are supplemented in some cases with more accurate or literal translations using notes. Readers will find that all the Anishinaabemowin terms Pokagon uses in his birch bark stories are accompanied by notes with context on translation and modern spelling provided by Malott. In the notes, he uses the Potawatomi-language writing system that was developed in 2012 in Crandon, Wisconsin, by the Forest County Potawatomi. Finally, light revisions were made to Pokagon's writing in cases of clear misspelling or "typos" in the printing process or misplaced capitalizations and mistakenly repeated words.

While each chapter of this volume that corresponds to one of Pokagon's birch bark books includes a book cover scan of the original text for the respective chapter, editing restrictions prohibited us from reproducing the scans of every page of the birch bark book collection here. However, the Pokagon Band of Potawatomi hosts an online archive called *Wiwkwébthëgen*, meaning "bundle" or "place where sacred items are stored." Visitors to the website can see complete scans of the birch bark book collection by visiting http://wiwkwebthegen.com. The digitizations include every page of the books, cover to cover, and can be found by navigating to "Documents" and clicking "Douglas Fisher Collection" under the "Collections" filter.

Notes

1. Personal communication with Blaire Morseau, January 14, 2022.
2. Margaret Noori, "Reading *Queen of the Woods* Today," in Pokagon, *Ogimawkwe Mitigwaki* (*Queen of the Woods*) (East Lansing: Michigan State University Press, 2011), 57.

Introduction

Bmejwen Kyle Malott and Blaire Morseau

Carefully enveloped between protective acid-free folders and locked behind the heavy door of a chilly archives room on the Pokagon Band of Potawatomi tribal lands in southwest Michigan are four peculiar little birch bark books. Their small size—fitting in the palm of one's hand—and the thinness of the paper bound with over one-hundred-year-old green silk ribbon is a deceptive performance of delicacy and fragility. It is deceptive because these books made from thin layers of the bark of white birch trees are indeed strong and durable. As the author himself proclaims, "this most remarkable tree with manifold bark [was] used by us instead of paper, being of greater value to us as it could not be injured by sun or water." Thus, when visitors to the Pokagon Band archive show an anxious precaution in their handling of these small books, as if a mere touch will cause them to disintegrate, one cannot help but be amused.

The republication of all four of Simon Pokagon's birch bark book titles that you hold—*The Pottawatamie Book of Genesis: Legend of the Creation of Man, Algonquin Legends of Paw Paw Lake, Algonquin Legends of South Haven*, and *The Red Man's Rebuke*—follow the 2011 edition of his most notable work, the novel *Ogimawkwe Mitigwaki* (*Queen of the Woods*), a love story and temperance work of fiction inspired by Pokagon's life experiences.[1] Much has changed in the southwest Michigan Potawatomi community of which Simon Pokagon was a part since *Queen of the Woods* was originally published in 1899 by his attorney, C. H. Engle, shortly after Pokagon's death. And much has changed since its republication just one decade ago. When *Queen of the Woods* was reprinted in 2011 by Michigan State University Press, the Pokagon Band of Potawatomi Indians—for whom Simon Pokagon is a historical patriarch—had no dedicated space for proper storage of archives or collections like the one mentioned in the opening of this essay. In fact, the Department of Language and Culture (now Center for History and Culture) where all four of the original birch bark book titles in this collection are presently accessioned did not even exist as a unique department yet. Services and programming that would later form the work of Language and Culture were still elements of the Education Department for the tribal government.

With the establishment of the first tribally owned casino in 2007, the Pokagon Band has dramatically increased its institutional and political power and has established itself as a significant blip on the mental radars of the non-Native populace in the region—departing from the decades-long invisibility of Native peoples in Michigan.[2] With a team of eleven employees servicing the community through workshops, classes, presentations, and more, and with a brand-new building to host such programming, the Department of Language and Culture has attracted the attention of local non-Native collectors of Indigenous material culture.[3] As a result, in 2016 an elderly man sold his collection of Simon Pokagon materials to the Band—a collection now referred to as the Douglas Fisher Collection—which he had spent much of his life acquiring. This Douglas Fisher Collection includes some of Pokagon's other publications in various periodicals, such as his account of the massacre of Fort Dearborn in *Harper's New Monthly Magazine* (1899) as well as, of course, the original birch bark books.

One of those birch bark books, the *Red Man's Greeting* (an alternative title to *The Red Man's Rebuke*), is accessioned in some of the most prestigious institutions in the country, such as the Newberry Library in Chicago. Yet little to nothing is written about Pokagon's three other birch bark books. *The Pottawatamie Book of Genesis: Legend of the Creation of Man*, *Algonquin Legends of Paw Paw Lake*, and *Algonquin Legends of South Haven* have been obscured by history, perhaps due to disinterest from historians and scholars of early Native literature and Indigenous studies, or perhaps due to the rare availability of these texts. Whatever the cause, the birch bark books—both as a collection and on their own—are critical sources of nineteenth-century Indigenous intellectual thought. The content of Pokagon's writing insists on the validity of Indigenous spiritual beliefs, the importance of creation stories, as well as the love of land in the context of extreme dispossession and a particular brand of American racism informed by the late-nineteenth-century eugenics movement. More than the sum of its parts, however, Pokagon's texts are not just a quaint series that laments cultural and environmental loss. Instead, the birch bark books leverage Indigenous agency and make space for Neshnabék in the future, and thus constitute important interventions in Native literary studies and critical Indigenous theory.[4] Pokagon's birch bark books enact what coauthor of this introduction Blaire Morseau has described elsewhere as Neshnabé futurisms or "Indigenous-made speculative film, art, video games, literature, and oral storytelling that draws from autochthonous knowledge systems to envision and convey alternative futurisms and pasts to mainstream ones with Indigenous communities at the forefront of this imaginary landscape."[5] But before unpacking this term and its application to the books, who was Simon Pokagon and what was his role in the larger Indigenous community of the nineteenth-century Great Lakes region?

Simon Pokagon was the son of Odawa/Ojibwe leader Sakiwnik, also known as Pokagon and baptized Leopold Pokagon. Simon's mother was Ketesse, baptized Elizabeth Topinabee, the daughter of Potawatomi leader Topinabee. A complicated figure, Simon Pokagon is often referred to in early twentieth-century texts and periodicals as "the Last Hereditary Chief of the Potawatomi." Indeed, some of the birch bark books are ascribed to "Chief Pokagon." Customarily, however, Potawatomi communities have complex, traditionally defined leadership roles, and hereditary chief is not one of them.[6] What is more, his notoriety marked him as somewhat of a "showboat" by other Potawatomis, because they felt Pokagon masqueraded Indianness to curious Victorian White folks, most famously at the 1893 Columbian Exposition, where he spoke. While Simon's father, Leopold Pokagon, protected his village from relocation in the 1830s and politically advocated for his community in the 1833 Treaty of Chicago, the current name of the Band as Pokagon is not free from controversy. Marcus Winchester, former director of the Pokagon Band Department of Language and Culture, once told Morseau that in the late 1980s and early '90s when the

Pokagon Band was on the cusp of federal recognition that "Even back then, folks were still asking, 'Well, why do we gotta name ourselves *Pokagon*?'"[7] The tribe had gone by several titles, such as the Catholic Potawatomi of the Saint Joseph River Valley and the Potawatomi Indian Nation Inc. (PINI) throughout the twentieth century, in addition to the endonyms Neshnabék and Bodwéwadmik.[8] The name Pokagon Band indexes the important political work Leopold Pokagon did for the tribe. However, due to some of the actions of his son, Simon, as well as to long-held family politics and conflicts, the surname Pokagon remains a somewhat controversial title for our tribe even today.[9]

Nonetheless, Simon Pokagon was an important intellectual, activist, and writer. He was born sometime in 1830 near Bertrand and died on January 28, 1899, in Hartford, Michigan.[10] He married Lonidaw Angeline, for whom he dedicated his most famous work, *Ogimawkwe Mitigwaki*, or *Queen of the Woods*. Pokagon's writing resisted common misconceptions about Native Americans such as labels of savagery and Godlessness, advocated for the rights of the environment, and reclaimed Indigenous space in Michigan and throughout the Great Lakes in ways that still permeate history to affect readers of his texts today. Because he was a prolific writer and Native American activist, Pokagon spoke at the 1893 World's Columbian Exposition as an invited lecturer and even built a birch bark wigwam at the fair.[11] As in his writings, he spoke about loss of land, racial and religious injustice, treaty rights, and advocated for Native American religious thought and logic systems to be treated by non-Native society as equally valid as those of the Western world.

He did all this on small, thin birch bark paper carefully peeled from white birch trees, split by hand into smaller leaflets, cut into pocket-sized squares, and curiously prepared for the printing press—a thoroughly obscure process until Wisecup's research published in this volume. The materiality of this birch bark is remarkable in form and function. As Berliner (2010) writes, "the grain on the pages is lighter than the printed text, the words appear to be behind the grain of the wood. The visual effect is three-dimensional, as though the words were emanating from within the bark."[12] Indeed reading Pokagon's prose significantly elevates the standard experience of reading bound books, making the feeling of handling the birch bark books a poetic one in and of itself. The reason Pokagon chose to print his stories and oral histories on birch paper was not just a creative or aesthetic rationale, but a political one. His books pay homage to traditional uses of birch paper for the Potawatomi:

> My object in publishing the Red Man's Rebuke on the bark of the white birch tree, is out of loyalty to my own people. . . . Out of this wonderful tree were made hats, caps and dishes for domestic use, while our maidens tied with it the knot that sealed their marriage vow; wigwams were made of it, as well as large canoes that outrode the violent storms on lake and sea; it was also used for light and fuel at our war councils and spirit dances. Originally the shores of our northern lakes and streams were fringed with it and evergreen, and white charmingly contrasted with the green mirrored from the water was indeed beautiful, but like the red man this tree is vanishing from our forests.[13]

While not explicitly mentioned in his texts, Pokagon's use of birch paper to print his works also hints at traditional birch bark scrolls used by Neshnabék across the Great Lakes. Those scrolls were and continue to be used by ceremony leaders to transcribe oral histories, stories, ceremonial knowledge, and other valuable information of Neshnabé ceremonial and historical life through pictographs, most notably in the Midéwiwin society.

Pokagon's texts tell stories that add a richness to the understanding of where the tribe came from as Neshnabék. He reminds readers, who were largely non-Native when these were first published and sold as souvenirs, of the original Indigenous place names that they now occupy. One important example is *Zhegagosh* or Chicago, meaning the place of wild onions, leeks, or ramps.[14] Another is "Ki-tchi-git-a-gan" referenced in *Algonquin Legends of Paw Paw Lake* and translated by him as "earthly paradise." In using this linguistic construction, Pokagon also leverages the events, stories, and traditional knowledge tied to those names in his writings. In that sense, he reclaims Indigenous places in Michigan that have erased the Native presence from areas such as South Haven (a place referred to by Potawatomi people traditionally as *Nikonêng*, or "Beautiful Sunset") and Niles (referred to by Potawatomis as *N'dowawjoyêk* [Dowagiac], meaning "Place of Harvesting").

Simon Pokagon's birch bark books tell the stories of the Pokagon Band of Potawatomi Indians that, as a result of their being accessioned in the tribe's archives, serve to reacquaint tribal members with their ancestors, traditional knowledge, and homeland. At the same time, though, Pokagon's writings refute American settlement and ecological destruction in a time when Native peoples had little to no agency to do so. In *The Red Man's Rebuke* [to the World's Fair] for example, Pokagon states, "No; sooner would we hold high joy-day over the graves of our departed fathers, than to celebrate our own funeral, the discovery of America." The 1893 Chicago World's Fair, also called the Columbian Exposition, was a grand celebration of the four hundred years since Christopher Columbus's "discovery" of America. Hundreds of nations and communities of people across the globe were represented through performance, food, souvenirs, exhibits, and dioramas (sometimes the exhibits included living human beings on display). Columbus's genocidal invasion aside, the 1893 celebration of the transatlantic trade that would make empire possible and birth the United States as a young settler colonial project is something Pokagon and other Indigenous peoples would no sooner "hold high joy-day over the graves of our departed fathers, than to celebrate our own funeral, the discovery of America."

In addition to refusing the celebration of settler colonialism, Pokagon also centers Indigenous philosophy as, at the very least, equal to that of Christianity. In *The Pottawatamie Book of Genesis* (a tongue-in-cheek title) and in *Algonquin Legends of Paw Paw Lake*, Pokagon notes that "tradition [is] as sacred to us as Holy Writ to the White man," making an argument for the validity of Neshnabé oral traditions as equal to that of the written history of Christians. Finally, another comment worth noting is Pokagon's lithographic sketch of "Chicago in my grandfather's day," which depicts dozens of conical wigwams where the city is now. This last example exposes "The Great White City"[15] as once an important crossroads of many Native communities that used to gather and trade in that place called *Zhegagoynak*, or the place of wild onions.[16]

Chicago is an inherently Indigenous place, an ancestral as well as contemporary home to many tribes beyond the Potawatomi, and the fact that Simon Pokagon not only sold *The Red Man's Rebuke* but spoke at the 1893 World's Fair is of no small consequence. Why did Pokagon decide to include the image of Chicago from his grandfather's day in *The Red Man's Rebuke*? The coauthor of this introduction, Bmejwen Kyle Malott, considering the linguistic heterogeneity of what is referred to as the Potawatomi language, explains how Sauk influences, the use of occasional Odawa words, and Ojibwe phrasing parallel the very real historical, biological, and cultural heterogeneity of Algonquian-speaking peoples in the Great Lakes region. The fact that Simon was of "mixed" heritage—Odawa, Ojibwe, and Potawatomi—was not an exception to Indigenous life, but a rule. As historian Richard White explains, "tribal designations . . . should be understood largely as ethnic rather than political or even cultural designations. The meaningful political unit . . . is the village, and Indian villages usually contained members of several tribes."[17] So, one can safely imagine Menominee, Myaamia, Potawatomi, Ojibwe peoples and more in the artistic rendition of Indigenous Chicago featured in *The Red Man's Rebuke*.[18] If we can imagine Simon Pokagon's grandfather (if indeed he meant his father's father), that would place this imagery at about the mid-1700s. By this loosely defined time frame, explorers like René-Robert Cavelier (Sieur de La Salle), Jesuit priests like Father Claude Jean Allouez, and other European actors were traveling through the Chicago region, the larger *Pays d'en Haut*, and the even greater still region of the Midwest for the past one hundred years, interacting, trading, fighting, and allying with tribes and sometimes taking Indigenous spouses. The image of Chicago in Pokagon's grandfather's day would have been a multilayered fabric of intertribal political alliances with the results of European political and economic industry folded into eighteenth-century Indigenous experiences.

As an example of the ways in which Indigenous peoples of the Great Lakes have always shared political, cultural, and biological ties, Simon Pokagon was the son of Leopold Pokagon and Elizabeth Topinabee. Leopold Pokagon was born to Odawa and Ojibwe parents while Elizabeth Topinabee was born to Potawatomi parents. The contemporary tribal identities of Potawatomi, Odawa, and Ojibwe—collectively known as Neshnabé or Anishinaabe—share similarities in language and culture.[19] This is because the Neshnabé migration story describes how they were all one people at one time. Before traveling back to the Great Lakes region via the Saint Lawrence seaway somewhere around 1,100 AD, the Potawatomi, Odawa, and Ojibwe lived together on the East Coast in the present-day area of New Brunswick and Maine. As a result, the languages of the dozen or so bands of Potawatomi, seven bands of Ojibwe (also spelled Ojibwa and Chippewa), and the few bands of Odawa (also spelled Ottawa) in the United States and Canada are all related but have evolved into their own unique political and linguistic identities.

In everyday use, one will notice influences from other languages in each, depending on which tribes were traditionally close by. For instance, Potawatomi has influence from the Sauk language, one example being the Potawatomi word *miktthéwi* (he or she works); the Ojibwe equivalent, *anoki* (he or she works), has no relation to the Potawatomi word, but if you look at the Sauk word *mîhkechêwîwa* (he or she works) you will find the influence. In the contemporary language used by the Pokagon Band of Potawatomi Indians you will also find Myaamia (also spelled Miami) influence as there are citizens who carry Myaamia surnames, an example being Topash. When you dig back into history you will find a lot of intermarriage, one example being an ancestor of Topinabee, an eighteenth/nineteenth-century Potawatomi leader in Michigan. Topinabee's great grandfather was known as Kendawa; in the Myaamia language *kintiwa* translates to golden eagle. Another thing to look at when reading Pokagon's entries are the stark differences in the orthography or writing systems. The first encounter we see in *Pottawatamie Book of Genesis*, for example, is "Ki-ji Man-i-to" (The Great Spirit). Indeed, Pokagon uses Ki-ji Man-i-to quite often throughout all four birch bark books. The interesting thing here is that the first vowel sound in "man-i-to" is something that is consistent in Odawa and Ojibwe, but not Potawatomi; that version is *mnedo* (spirit) and *ktthémnedo* or *gzhémnedo*, the latter two meaning "great" or "powerful" spirit. For Ojibwe and Odawa speakers, the word for Great Spirit is pronounced in a way that emphasizes individual syllables—slowly and deliberately. The Potawatomi spelling and pronunciation, on the other hand, flows much faster and there is less emphasis on the middle syllables.

The next notable examples of language or dialect mixing are Pokagon's use of "nomash," which he translates as fish, and "ni-bi-nong" which he translates as "the waters." This is another curious example, because Potawatomi, Odawa, and Ojibwe all use the word *gigo* for fish. Malott thinks what he is saying is that there are *namés* or little sturgeon. It's possible Pokagon used that word because in the specific area of southwest Michigan where Pokagon lived, when someone says they are Fish Clan, it is actually the sturgeon that they are referring to specifically, hence the use of "nomash" or "names" as it is spelled today. Furthermore, the locative ending "nong" in the place name "ni-bi-nong" is consistent with Ojibwe and Odawa. Next, Pokagon uses "b-nes-sig" and "no-din," which he translates to "the fowls" and "the air" respectively. These examples are still used in all three languages. At the beginning of *Algonquin Legends of Paw Paw Lake*, Pokagon uses "bi-bon-og nin-go-twak" and translates that to "a hundred years ago." Another way one can say that would be *égi ngotwak pongék*—literally meaning one hundred years ago. Readers will come across "sa-gi-i-gan" for "lake," which is also used in Potawatomi, Odawa, and Ojibwe, but its use has been in decline in Potawatomi in the last two hundred years.

The Potawatomi version of the word is *zagen*. He then uses "Au-nish-a-naw-beg" for "the Indians." This use of the word is the Ojibwe version, which is currently written as *Anishinaabeg* or Anishinaabek. The Odawa version is *Nishnaabek*, and the Potawatomi version is *Neshnabék*. Later on, Pokagon uses "au-ne-ne gaje ik-we" for man and woman—the use of these forms is definitely of Ojibwe origin and currently spelled *inini gaye ikwe*. The Potawatomi do not use "gaye" for the word "and," but instead use the word *miné*. So, the term combination would be *nėnė minė kwé* in Potawatomi.

It is unclear whether Pokagon's translations from the Indigenous utterances into English were ever meant to be literal. For example, in *Algonquian Legends of South Haven* Pokagon uses "Ki-tchi-git-a-gan" as "earthly paradise." Malott notes that this is a largely romanticized translation, as *ktthe gtegan* literally means "a big garden." There are also missing linguistic possessives in Pokagon's writing. The first instance in *Legends* of language use is when Pokagon translated "ki-os-ag" as "our forefathers." This is a particularly poignant example because it is missing an important particle to mean *ours*. "Ki-os-ag" *or gosêk/kosêk* means *your* fathers; in order for it to mean *our* fathers it would have to have "nan" from the word *ginan* or "us" in it: *gosnanêk/kosnanêk* is the correct form of "our fathers." It would be extremely odd for a nineteenth-century person who grew up speaking Potawatomi or even Ojibwe or Odawa to make this mistake unless Pokagon was experiencing significant language regression. He then uses the word "maw-kaw-te" and translates that into Black River. In Ojibwe *makade*, and *mkedé* in Potawatomi both just mean "black." In order to refer to this river you would need to say *mkedé zibé* or Black River.

Would a person who has spent their entire lives speaking this Indigenous language make such glaring mistakes? Perhaps these errors are the result of poor editing, or, as mentioned earlier, Pokagon's language had regressed quite a bit due to settler influence at the time of writing. Whatever the case, such lackadaisical translations and awkward grammatical blunders have led some audiences to speculate that Pokagon had a ghostwriter, or at the very least, a heavy-handed editor who was not fluent in Anishinaabe languages.

Next, he uses "An-a-kan" for Rush Lake. An-a-kan or *anaakan* in Ojibwe and *naken* in Potawatomi is the word for a rug or mat. It derives from the plant we used to make mats from *nagnesh* (great bulrush), hence the lake in Michigan being named "Rush Lake." The term we use for Rush Lake today is *nagneshkëmbes* (lake of the bulrush). He then uses "Wawbi-gan" as Swan Lake, now called Van Auken Lake. In Potawatomi *wabgen* translates to something that is used to make things white; this can refer to white clay, for example. In this context, however, Malott has heard *wabzhi mbes* to more accurately reference "swan lake." Another curious instance of linguistic form is where Pokagon uses "o-de-na-wan" for "Indian villages." This form as well as the alternative spelling, *odanwan*, is actually a possessive form meaning "*their* villages." Later he uses "Mo-o-se" for an elk; this is interesting because all three languages use different forms of *moz* or *mozo* for a moose, suggesting this is also where the English word comes from. The most common word for an elk is in fact *mzhéwé*. Pokagon then uses "maw-qui" for a bear, whereas the current words for the three languages are *mko* (Potawatomi), *mkwa* (Odawa), and *makwa* (Ojibwe).

The last thing Malott points out in this story is towards the end, where Pokagon uses "ni-kig, es-i-can, and aw-mik" for "the otter, coon, and beaver." The use of "ni-kig" is *ngig* in Odawa and *nigig* in Ojibwe, but the Potawatomi word for an otter is *gdedé*. For a racoon, the Ojibwe say *esiban*, the Odawa say *esban*, and the Potawatomi say *éspen*. As for beaver, the Ojibwe use *amik*, the Odawa use *mik*, and the Potawatomi use *mëk*.

Next Pokagon uses "Ish-pem-ing," meaning "a high place." This is the Ojibwe spelling of what in Potawatomi is *shpëmëk*, meaning "up high" or "in the sky"—referring to Ishpeming, Michigan, named after the Ojibwe word (the Odawa version is *shpiming*). After this he then uses "ki-tchi-tchang" as "his soul," which is curious because this is another Ojibwe word currently written as *jichaag*, or "a soul." Potawatomi and Odawa use versions of *thibéy* and *jibe* respectively. The use of "mit-ig-wad" for "bow" Malott believes to just be a typo, since *mtegwap* or *mtegwab* is the word for a bow.

Lastly, in *The Red Man's Rebuke* Pokagon uses primarily English instead of Anishinaabemowin, but in creative and strategic ways. In their traditional arrangement, Neshnabé villages in the Great Lakes were not comprised of only one tribe, but of multiple tribes. Other organizing principles like clan affiliations would have influenced the locality of our ancestors much more than the European concept of "tribe." Even after settler encroachment in the Great Lakes and the subsequent statehoods that further dispossessed Indigenous peoples of their lands and traditions, there were multiple tribes who continued to intermarry and related to each other in traditional ways. All of this is to say that while interesting and at times confusing, Simon Pokagon's use of all three languages (four if one includes English) in his writing is not surprising, but in fact, expected.

Understanding the complex heterogeneity of both linguistic use and village life in the eighteenth century that Pokagon indexes with his unique use of Anishinaabemowin, as well as the inclusion of the image of Indigenous Chicago referenced earlier in this introduction is important for understanding how he and others after him imagine Indigenous futurities. Despite hundreds of years of settler colonialism that tried and continues to try to erase Indigenous peoples, in part by incorrectly organizing them into "tribes" that stifle their agency and sense of larger nationhood, Potawatomi peoples and other related Neshnabék communities see themselves as close relatives. Potawatomi, Odawa, and Ojibwe communities across the continent of North America are at once related linguistically, biologically, culturally, politically, and spiritually beyond even what the commonly referenced Three Fires Confederacy conveys. There are no clean lines defining what is and what is not Potawatomi culture, at least not in the "intertribal" village life of the Great Lakes region before, during, or after Pokagon's writing. While this argument is not meant to dissolve into nihilism about Potawatomi identity or culture, it does complicate what many scholars have incorrectly assumed about Indigenous realities of the past and present.

Whether anthropologists attempt to define (essentialize) or expand ideas about the whole of a community's identity through observation and theorization, they're engaging in what James Elkin calls "mending the zeitgeist."[20] Georg Hegel (and those who later used his work) is responsible for contemporary understandings of culture or zeitgeist, which can be defined as the sum of the shared norms, beliefs, worldviews, and the expressions of those components through performance, language, and material culture of a community. But as Maureen Matthews eloquently explains in her scholarly work with another Neshnabé community in Canada, "A more useful cultural metaphor might be that of an Ojibwe archipelago, islands of Ojibwe experience amidst a sea of what most native people think of as 'dominant culture.' Waves of European understanding and practice . . . wash the beach of each unique Ojibwe reality."[21] And as Potawatomi, Odawa, and Ojibwe villages in the Great Lakes region were displaced; formally removed, as was the case for the Prairie Band in Kansas and the Citizen Band in Oklahoma; or managed to stay in their homelands, such as Leopold Pokagon's villages in southwest Michigan and Northern Indiana, Potawatomi realities have been recalibrated to fit new circumstances. Creation stories like the one Simon Pokagon shares continue to be told, and identities are forged despite American settlement, racism, and genocide in ways that ultimately form a meaningful set of Potawatomi notions of nationhood.[22]

Coauthor of this introduction, Morseau engages with Pokagon's writing and with ideas of Potawatomi identity that resist an overwhelming surge of ethnographic thought that has been damaging to Native peoples. In Morseau's training as an anthropologist, she has been obligated to engage with and cite ethnographies produced about Native peoples that have rarely been used to help their communities, and indeed have often resulted in crisis narratives that pathologize people of color or participated in their dispossession.[23] More specifically, the discipline of anthropology was formed in large part by ethnographers who have always thought about Indigenous peoples in temporalizing ways. Lewis Henry Morgan's *Ancient Society* posited three stages of cultural evolution—from savagery, barbarism, to civilization.[24] Placing human societies on a linear scale, Native peoples in North America were seen by White society, and for some continue to be seen, as relics of the past—contemporary groups of peoples living as one might expect Western peoples to have lived centuries earlier. Of course, this was an inaccurate and racist hierarchy of organizing humanity that anthropology has long since rejected. As the field of cultural anthropology developed in the United States, however, salvage ethnographic projects increased. These scholarly and political projects aimed to collect and preserve linguistic and material culture from Indigenous communities with the pervasive assumption that Native Americans would not exist in the future. Despite decades of rigorous scholarship and an institutional rejection of understanding human diversity in terms of biological evolutionary principles, Indigenous peoples are still affected by these problematic temporalizing theories.

Insolent ideas of "primitive" versus "modern" cultures would permeate peoples' understanding of humanity for decades. As such, these dubious understandings of cultural difference would legitimize policies aimed at "civilizing" Native American peoples. The calamitous effects of policies of cultural genocide such as Native American boarding schools, and land theft as a result of policies like the Dawes Act of 1887 on Native Americans cannot be overstated. Because much has been published on this topic, the project of this introduction to Pokagon's birch bark stories is not to add to this important discussion. Rather, we are attentive to the ways that Indigenous futurisms have made new spaces for Indigenous peoples in the future, particularly through language, material culture, and stewardship in tribally owned archives.

Indigenous futurisms is a conceptual rejection of theoretical, institutional, and political projects that placed Indigenous peoples in the past or framed Indigenous peoples as trying to rectify their place in the modern present. The content of Pokagon's publications stakes claim to space in the past and in the future, while the material of the books—birch bark—makes implicit references to birch bark scrolls used in Midéwiwin ceremonies. Pokagon lamented the loss of *wigwas* or white paper birch trees, particularly in *The Red Man's Rebuke*. He argues that as a result of White settlement and urban development, the white birch trees once "charmingly contrasted with the green mirrored from the water was indeed beautiful, but like the red man this tree is vanishing from our forests." One could certainly write off Pokagon's lament as informed by, if not completely influenced by, Victorian rhetoric of the "vanishing Indian" or peddling a Native version of Uncle Tom for personal notoriety or financial gain.[25] More than this, however, there are contemporary parallels to the environmental and political regimes that inform Simon Pokagon's texts that are important to highlight here.

The ecological circumstances that Simon Pokagon witnessed, together with his frustrations ensconced in his writing style, lend themselves to a Neshnabék historical as well as contemporary zeitgeist related to climate change and growing Indigenous resistance movements. Nineteenth-century Michigan underwent some of the most dramatic and devastating surface topography and ecological changes in North America—from draining wetlands for settlers' farms to channelizing meandering waterways to transport millions of timber logs from clear-cutting ventures. While the Pokagon Band community is descended from those villages not removed from their original homelands, the dispossession experienced by those Potawatomis in the 1800s violently excluded them from their land, natural resources, ancestors, and ways of life. With this context in mind, Pokagon's writing is prophetic, incorporates traditional stories, and served to call attention to concurrent environmental issues he and his community experienced all while refusing to be erased. Instead of consenting to the trope of the "vanishing Indians," his books deploy iterations of Indigenous futurisms that collapse time in ways that activist and Lakota historian Nick Estes explains as departing from settler notions of time. Settler ideas and constructions of history organize events in a linear fashion in order to distance themselves from the uncomfortable realities of violence wrought against Native peoples and our ecologies. He further explains that "Indigenous notions of time consider the present to be structured entirely by our past and by our ancestors." He continues, "There is no separation between past and present, meaning that an alternative future is also determined by an understanding of our past."[26] In other words, major historical events, Indigenous social movements, and other iterations of what we may understand as separate historical "moments" from Pontiac's Rebellion to the Ghost Dance and even the NoDAPL camps at Standing Rock are not isolated events that have a beginning and an end. These events or occurrences are instead nodes or entanglements of past, present, and future that just happen to erupt in legible ways. Indigenous conceptions of time are entangled and circular in webs of relationships between humans, the land, and other-than-human beings—continuous social threads that are always related to the past and future.

When looking to material culture, for instance, "epitomizing objects" defined by Matthews as an object's "social force, their agency within their own biographical narrative, their participation in multiple biographies, and the way in which they appear to have the social role of persons," we thought of the effects items have on their makers, keepers, and inheritors.[27] Like Pokagon's books, another item from the Pokagon Band archives illustrates this point well. It is an unfinished sketch (unfinished because it was never made into a painting) by nineteenth-century landscape and portrait artist George Winter labeled "Kee-waw-nay Village, 1837." Winter spent several months in the summer of 1837 sketching the doings of Potawatomi peoples in northern Indiana and writing about them in his journals. His amateur ethnographic material resulted in dozens of paintings, journal entries, and letters about Potawatomi peoples in Northern Indiana during the Removal era. While Morseau worked at the Pokagon Band in the role of archivist in late 2017 to August 2019, she followed the nuanced interpretations given to this artifact by the former tribal historic preservation officer Jason S. Wesaw, and the former director of Language and Culture Marcus Winchester. What they pointed out to visitors as notable and

FIGURE 1. Sketch by George Winter (1837) of Kee-waw-nay Village (present-day La Porte, Indiana, near Bruce's Lake), Center for History and Culture, Dowagiac, 2016.6.1.

unique about the sketch was important for understanding contemporary religious politics in the tribe, as well as hinting at what our individual ideals for Neshnabé religious identity *should* be.

These imaginaries of Potawatomi spiritual life are important in light of the Band's history in relation to removal. Advocating for his village as legibly "civilized" by Euro-American standards of Christianity, Western-style agricultural practices, and speaking English, Leopold Pokagon was able to negotiate a provision in the 1833 Treaty of Chicago that removed hundreds of other Native communities. The extent of Christian adoption and reliance on English in everyday life has been debated by the Pokagon community even to this day. Some argue that these "Catholic Potawatomis" adopted the religion for political reasons only, while others argue that these social changes were a welcome byproduct of larger processes of assimilation.[28] As a tribe whose history has often been brutally chalked up to "We converted to Christianity, so we got to stay," contemporary Potawatomi traditionalists often roll their eyes, knowing that our history is much more complicated than that.[29]

Jason, a member of the Three Fires Midéwiwin Lodge, would quickly point out what he perceived to be a water drum in the sketch.[30] While not everyone agrees that the instrument in the sketch is in fact a water drum, his observation was not inconsequential. A water drum or "Little Boy Water Drum" is used in Midéwiwin ceremonies. In fact, in a breakdown of the Potawatomi spelling of Midéwiwin, *Mdwéwen* refers to the sounds of something (*mdwé*: the sound something makes). So, while Midéwiwin is often translated as "medicine"—and indeed there are many healing and medicinal components to the lodge, Midéwiwin references the sound of the water drum used in ceremony. So, if Wesaw is correct, the depiction of a Little Boy Water Drum in a sketch from 1837 indicates that Potawatomi people were still practicing Midéwiwin or Midéwiwin-adjacent ceremonies at that time.

Contemporary Neshnabé politics and identities tied to religion collapse time because these politico-identities make space for Indigenous agency in the past and in the future. These ceremonial elements included in primary documents are important to Pokagon citizens who identify as traditionalists (i.e., usually meaning non-Christian even if they are not formally a member of any ceremonial lodge such as Big Drum, Midéwiwin, or other). As the George Winter sketch was made in 1837, it is dated to post-Removal in a time when supposedly all Potawatomis still living in the northern Indiana and southern Michigan area had converted to Catholicism in order to stay in their homelands.

In antiquity, villages and communities who would later become different bands of Potawatomi Indians in Michigan and Indiana were referred to as the Catholic Potawatomi of the Saint Joseph River Valley. Today, however, the nearly six thousand enrolled citizens of the Pokagon Band alone (not considering the other Potawatomi bands in Michigan or elsewhere) are religiously diverse. Like many tribal communities, there are politics of Catholicism or Christianity more generally on the one hand and traditionalists (mostly Midéwiwin, but some Big Drum members) on the other. And there are some who claim they walk "in both worlds." The nuances of everyday religious life, as well as how Christianity has affected what are now viewed as "traditional" Potawatomi practices, are much more complicated than the "two worlds" view. But this is how many Pokagons understand this religious complexity nonetheless. As a result, Christian Potawatomi folks will often explain Leopold Pokagon's leadership as one that valued Catholicism and the Potawatomis' historic relationship with French Jesuits in the 1600s and 1700s. Those who identify as traditional will instead see Leopold's resistance against removal and public espousal of Catholicism as a series of creative strategies to allow his villages to remain in their traditional homelands.

The unfinished sketch, like Pokagon's birch bark books that contain Christian prose as well as elements of resistance and refusal, complicates what many Pokagons, especially those practicing Catholicism, accept as our ancestors' politico-religious historical narrative (e.g., the loosely quoted historical synopsis earlier, which implies that the Pokagon villagers were Christian "sell-outs"). While we cannot hope to fully understand the hearts and minds of our nineteenth-century ancestors, what is clear is that Simon Pokagon's texts are not just a quaint series of nineteenth-century literature that lament cultural and environmental loss. Rather, the birch bark books leverage Indigenous agency and make space for Neshnabék in the future on our own terms. In other words, they enact what Morseau has described elsewhere as Neshnabé futurisms or Indigenous-made media such as film, art, video games, literature, and oral storytelling that draws from Indigenous knowledge systems to imagine alternative existences to mainstream ones with Indigenous peoples at the forefront of this speculative landscape.[31] Simon Pokagon's texts reconnect Potawatomi peoples to their land, the archives of knowledge held in those places despite centuries of dispossession by settler colonialism. As a consequence, the Neshnabé stories Pokagon shares with us have material effects on the possibilities Indigenous people envision for themselves while making space for Indigenous agency in the future, one that is "as sacred to us as Holy Writ to the White man."

Notes

1. *The Red Man's Rebuke* was also printed as *Red Man's Greeting*. See "A Note on the Texts" in this collection. Simon Pokagon, *Ogimawkwe Mitigwaki: Queen of the Woods* (East Lansing: Michigan State University Press, 2011).
2. This is due in no small part to the fact that many of the state's twelve federally recognized tribes were not reaffirmed until the 1990s.
3. During the preparation of this introduction, the Department of Language and Culture separated into two departments: the Center for History and Culture and the language program's Pokagon Ėthë Bodwéwadmimwat Department.
4. *Neshnabék* is the Potawatomi spelling of the more common Ojibwe spelling, *Anishinaabék*, meaning "true humans," "original people," or "those who were lowered down," the latter referencing the Anishinaabé creation story or the teaching regarding humanity's "low place" among other beings.
5. Blaire Topash-Caldwell, "'Beam Us Up, Bgwéthnéné!' Indigenizing Science (Fiction)," *AlterNative: An International Journal of Indigenous Peoples* 16, no. 2 (June 2020): 81–89.

6. Though hereditary chief was not a traditional role, it was not uncommon for the children of popular leaders to rise to a similar influential role in their respective communities. But leadership was not a birthright as compared to many European societies. See Cary Miller, *Ogimaag: Anishinaabeg Leadership, 1760–1845*, illustrated ed. (Lincoln: University of Nebraska Press, 2016).

7. Federal recognition of the Pokagon Band was reaffirmed in 1994.

8. The anglicized "Potawatomi" derives from *Bodwéwadmik*. Bodwéwadmi is the singular form of the plural Bodwéwadmik and refers to "s/he builds the fire."

9. There was also animosity toward the appointment of Leopold's son, Peter, as chief by Father Edward Sorin (founder of the University of Notre Dame). Due to a violation of traditional leadership roles and contextualized by severe dispossession and disenfranchisement, Father Sorin's appointment of Peter to chief of the Michigan village was highly problematic, to say the least.

10. Hartford, Michigan, was also known as *Byankik*, meaning "the place where we went" under the leadership of Singowa in 1850, after disagreements fractured Leopold's village in Silver Creek, Michigan.

11. For a discussion about this, see John N. Low, "The Architecture of Simon Pokagon—In Text and on Display," in *Ogimawkwe Mitigwaki (Queen of the Woods)* (East Lansing: Michigan State University Press, 2011), 1–30.

12. Jonathan Berliner, "Written in the Birch Bark: The Linguistic-Material Worldmaking of Simon Pokagon," *PMLA/Publications of the Modern Language Association of America* 125, no. 1 (January 2010): 73–91.

13. Simon Pokagon, *The Red Man's Rebuke* (Hartford, MI: C. H. Engle, 1893).

14. This is where the anglicized spelling of the city Chicago derives its name.

15. "Great White City" was a popular name for Chicago during the era of the 1893 World's Fair/Columbian Exposition.

16. The particle *-ak* is a locative that turns *Zhegagosh*, meaning wild onion or leek, into *Zhegagoynak*, meaning the place of wild onions or leeks.

17. Richard White, *The Middle Ground: Indians, Empires, and Republics in the Great Lakes Region, 1650–1815* (Cambridge: Cambridge University Press, 1991), 30.

18. This image is, unfortunately, too light and difficult to see if reproduced here.

19. *Anishinaabe* is the more commonly used Ojibwe spelling.

20. James Elkins, *Stories of Art*, 1st ed. (New York: Routledge, 2002). Also see James Clifford, *The Predicament of Culture* (Cambridge, MA: Harvard University Press, 1988).

21. Maureen Matthews, *Naamiwan's Drum: The Story of a Contested Repatriation of Anishinaabe Artefacts*, 1st ed. (Toronto: University of Toronto Press, 2016). For a description of cultural archipelago, see Alan C. Cairns, Jean Comaroff, and John Comaroff, "Ethnography and the Historical Imagination," *Journal of Interdisciplinary History* 25, no. 3 (1995): 456.

22. For more on Potawatomi nationhood, see Wetzel, *Gathering the Potawatomi Nation*, 1st ed. (Norman: University of Oklahoma Press, 2016).

23. For more on the damaging effects of anthropology, see Linda Tuhiwai Smith, *Decolonizing Methodologies: Research and Indigenous Peoples*, 2nd ed. (London: Zed Books, 2012); and Kyle Whyte, "Against Crisis Epistemology," in *Routledge Handbook of Critical Indigenous Studies*, ed. Brendan Hokowhitu et al., 1st ed. (New York: Routledge, 2020), 52–64.

24. Lewis Henry Morgan and Elisabeth Tooker, *Ancient Society* (Tucson: University of Arizona Press, 1985).

25. For a political and literary explanation of vanishing Indigeneity, see Jean M. O'Brien, *Firsting and Lasting: Writing Indians out of Existence in New England* (Minneapolis: University of Minnesota Press, 2010).

26. Nick Estes, *Our History Is the Future: Standing Rock versus the Dakota Access Pipeline, and the Long Tradition of Indigenous Resistance* (New York: Verso Books, 2019).

27. Matthews, *Naamiwan's Drum*.

28. Indeed, the village would have been removed like the other villages to Kansas or Oklahoma, as evidenced by Prairie Band and Citizen Band respectively.

29. Traditionalists practice more traditional spiritual beliefs and ceremonies as well as attend lodges such as Big Drum or Midéwiwin.

30. The drum can be seen on the far right of the sketch being played by a seated person, facing the dancers in the middle of the gathering.

31. Topash-Caldwell, "Beam Us Up, Bgwëthnėnė!"

A Note on the Texts

Kelly Wisecup

A comparison of many available copies of *The Red Man's Rebuke* and *The Red Man's Greeting*, specifically of the type, layout, spelling, and content, provides evidence of several printings. This comparison supports evidence in *Hartford Day Spring* newspaper articles that make reference to the booklets first being printed in 1893, and then to several reprintings taking place across the next decade. Due to COVID-19, I have not been able to travel to all of the libraries that hold a copy of the *Rebuke* or *Greeting*, so I have relied on librarians who sent scans of the copies held at their institutions or on already existing digital editions. There are a few copies I was unable to consult. In addition, as Marieka Kaye and Oa Sjoblom point out in their essay in this volume, a complete bibliographic description of the booklets should take into account the birch bark pages, in particular when the pages were harvested (the color of the pages is a clue as to the season in which they were harvested). The following essay is therefore a starting point rather than a complete description, and I hope it offers a starting point for future study of the different copies and printings.

Booklets titled either *The Red Man's Rebuke* or *The Red Man's Greeting* were being printed on the *Hartford Day Spring* presses in spring 1893, according

21

to newspaper articles published in March and May 1893.[1] An examination of copies of the *Rebuke* and *Greeting* reveals differences in title pages, copyright, dedication, and "by the author" pages, which suggest several reprintings after 1893. The seven copies of the *Greeting* I've been able to consult use the same type for the title, and they include the words: "1492–1892" to the left of the illustration and an image, possibly representing a wampum belt, between "1492" and "1892." There are some small differences among these copies: in the Newberry Library's copy of the *Greeting*, the illustration of the fox includes a small duckling present in no other copies I've consulted (unnumbered page between pages 10 and 11, Newberry copy). The Wolfsonian's copy of the *Greeting* is missing altogether the page featuring the illustrations of the fox and an eagle, with their corresponding verses (perhaps someone omitted the page of illustrations when binding that copy). And finally, several dedication pages differently capitalize the phrase "Defenders of our race" (the Newberry and Wolfsonian copies include a lower-case "d," while the Trinity College copy capitalizes the word).[2]

The twelve copies of the *Rebuke* I have been able to compare have considerable variation. I have identified four different typefaces and layouts for the title pages. One version features a border around the image of Columbus, which is justified on the right-hand side of the title page; a second is identical to the *Greeting* title page in layout and type; and two other versions feature no border and center the image, while using different type for the title. There are also three different typefaces and layouts used for the "by the author" page and for the copyright page. Six of the copies I have consulted misspell Roger Williams's name in the dedication page, rendering it "Rodger," and two copies misspell Pokagon's name on the copyright page, rendering it "Simom."

Some versions of the *Rebuke* do not include the title "Red Man's Rebuke" at the top of page 1 (Briscoe, University of Michigan copies, and Pokagon Band copies) and instead begin with the words "By Simon Pokagon, Pottawatomie Chief." One of the copies held at the Clements library features a reset page of engravings that includes only the image of the fox, omitting the deer that in other copies appears above the fox on that same page. Two copies of the *Rebuke*, one held at the Smithsonian Institution and another at the New York Public Library, include a woodcut illustration of Pokagon, labeled "Chief Simon Pokagon, Hartford, Mich" (the printer used a page left blank in other editions to add this illustration). The *Rebuke*'s dedication page usually does not include

Emma Sickels, although the NYPL copy of the *Rebuke* includes Sickels, using a dedication page layout also found in copies of the *Greeting*. In the copies of both the *Rebuke* and the *Greeting* I've consulted, pages numbered 2–16 (the pages featuring the text of the pamphlet) appear to be consistent in type and layout.[3] It is possible that Engle and Pokagon arranged for plates of these pages to be made, so that reprinting the pamphlets required resetting only the cover, dedication, by the author, title page, and some of the pages of illustrations. This seems like a large expense for a booklet initially created as ephemera, but Engle did have stereotyped plates for one of W. A. Engle's books of poetry made, and perhaps he did the same for Pokagon's booklets.[4]

The copies of the *Rebuke* (Smithsonian and NYPL) that share a title page typeface and layout with the *Greeting* suggest that these copies may all have been printed around the same time. The printer seems to have reset the type for a few pages, including the title page, where he replaced "Rebuke" with "Greeting," using the same typeface. In these copies of the *Rebuke*, Pokagon's first name is spelled "Simom." If these copies are from the first print run of the *Rebuke*, the printer would have reset this page for the *Greeting*, correcting the spelling error. He reset the dedication page as well, with the upper and lower case "d's" for "defenders" and with the addition of Emma Sickels's name in copies of the *Greeting*. For this edition of the *Rebuke*, the printer included a woodcut of Pokagon (these pages are blank in copies of the *Greeting*) and set the page bearing the engraving of the eagle so that the lines of text do not exceed the space of the illustration. It is possible that these copies of the *Rebuke* and of the *Greeting* were all printed in early May 1893, when Pokagon and Engle were preparing both pamphlets with the *Day Spring* printer in the two-week period between May 12 and 23. One detail that substantiates this theory is in the NYPL copy of the *Rebuke*: its dedication page (unlike all others of the *Rebuke* I've consulted) includes Sickels's name, which otherwise appears only in the *Greeting*. The printer may have taken one of the dedication pages from copies of the *Greeting* and added it to the *Rebuke*, later adding the illustration of Pokagon on the verso side of the dedication page. The misspelling of Pokagon's first name in these two copies of the *Rebuke* likewise suggests a first (possibly hasty) printing, later corrected (the error does not appear in other copies of either the *Rebuke* or *Greeting* that I've consulted).

Scholars have speculated that the addition of Sickels's name to the *Greeting* is a sign that printing began with the *Rebuke* and that the title page and dedication were later changed for the *Greeting*, after Sickels assisted in arranging for the booklets to circulate at the Columbian Exposition. The *Tribune*'s March 4 advertisement of the *Rebuke* substantiates this argument that it was the pamphlet printed first. But there is also a longer, more complex story to be told about the *Rebuke*. One edition of the *Rebuke* seems to have been printed in early 1893 with the aim of circulating that booklet—along with the *Greeting*—at the Columbian Exposition and the New York Press Club Fair, where Emma Sickels played a significant role in obtaining copies of both pamphlets for sale at the fair and arranging Pokagon's appearance in Chicago. Sickels does not seem to have been involved with the booklets' circulations after the fair, and accordingly, Pokagon and Engle may have decided to return to reprint the *Rebuke* later in the 1890s, rewording the dedication to remove Sickels's name. The remaining *Rebuke* variants were likely the result of reprintings after 1893. Archival evidence and Pokagon's and Engle's correspondence indicate that copies of the *Rebuke* were being recirculated (and possibly reprinted) in 1897, and they were definitely being reprinted as late as 1904 (after Pokagon's death). It is likely that the *Day Spring* printer—probably different people, given the frequent turnover of owners at the newspaper—reset the type for these later editions, possibly using newly available type purchased by a new owner of the paper.[5]

Pokagon and Engle also had printed several promotional materials that accompanied the pamphlets and still remain with some copies today. These include a small sheet featuring a "Brief History of Simon Pokagon," which Engle "certif[ied]" as accurate, and on the reverse side a photograph of Pokagon (Newberry Library). In addition, they had printed a small card featuring the photograph of Pokagon followed by the lines "Simon Pokagon, Pottawattamie Chief. Author of the Red Man's Columbian Greeting, printed in a Booklet made of the bark of the White Birch tree." There are at least two printings of this card (see Newberry and Williams copies, which suggest different typesettings). And after the fair, Pokagon and Engle circulated a promotional card featuring the photograph of Pokagon, an advertisement for the "Red Man's Columbian Greeting," and, on the reverse, an account of Pokagon's appearance at the fair (Wisconsin Historical Society).

Many pamphlets contain six illustrations, at least four of which appear in type specimen books published in the early 1890s (type specimen books offered metal type, including typefaces, headers, and illustrations, that printers could purchase at relatively inexpensive rates and reuse for different printing jobs).

The illustrations of the eagle, fox, deer, and of the Indigenous man wearing a headdress on the pamphlets' back cover each appear in type specimen books.[6] In other words, four of the pamphlets' illustrations are stock images, likely selected out of the type already available at the *Day Spring* office. The illustration of the Indigenous man located on the *Rebuke/Greeting*'s back cover reappears across Pokagon's five birch bark booklets, acting like a visual signature on the back cover of the *Rebuke/Greeting*, as well as on the back cover of *Algonquin Legends of Paw Paw Lake*, *Algonquin Legends of South Haven*, and *The Pottawattamie Book of Genesis.*

Notes

1. "Poem by an Indian Chief," *Chicago Tribune*, 4 March 1893, 9; and *Hartford Day Spring*, 12 May 1893, 8.
2. I consulted copies of the *Greeting* held at the Newberry Library, the Wolfsonian Library at Florida International University, Trinity College, Clarke Historical Library, the Beinecke, the Wisconsin Historical Society, and Williams College Libraries.
3. I consulted copies of the *Rebuke* held at the A. K. Smiley Public Library (Redlands, CA), Autry Museum Library and Archives, Bentley Historical Library, the Briscoe Center for American History at the University of Texas, the Chicago Historical Museum, the Clarke Historical Library, the Clements Library at the University of Michigan (two copies), the Elkhart (IN) Public Library, Pokagon Band archives, Rauner Special Collections at Dartmouth College, the Smithsonian Institution, and the New York Public Library.
4. The *Day Spring* reported that its printer was experimenting with making impressions from the plates for W. A. Engle's book at the same time that he was printing the *Rebuke/Greeting* in May 1893. Engle seems to have had the means and connections to work with large printing houses in addition to the *Day Spring*'s small office, and he may have drawn on those connections to make plates for Pokagon's pamphlets.
5. "The Redman's Rebuke," *News-Palladium*, 18 February 1904, 8.
6. See, for instance, *The Specimen Book of Types from Farmer, Little & Company: Rules, Cuts, Borders, etc.* (New York: Type Foundry and Printer's Warehouse, 1885).

A Brief Survey of Documenting the Potawatomi Language

Corinne Kasper

Creating our own culturally informed Potawatomi archive is a powerful exercise, its impact extended through generations to influence my generation—granting me and my fellow tribal citizens access to our ways across time; our deeply rooted epistemology. For this reason, I want to begin this edition, possibly your first reading, with a note on Simon Pokagon's command of language.

Pokagon's proficiency and eloquence as a writer cannot be questioned. As a stably multilingual speaker and writer, Pokagon's use of language is powerful. From a linguistic point of view, he inserts "Potawatomi" words into the literature. I use quotes to note that the Potawatomi Pokagon employs may not be Potawatomi in the strictest, most prescriptive sense. As noted by Malott and Morseau in this collection, Pokagon was ethnically Potawatomi, Ojibwe, and Odawa. The Indian language he uses is an Anishinaabemowin of sorts. His word choice and pronunciation, represented in the spelling system he opts for, is indicative of the Odawa language. Even the semantic particles he uses, such as *dash*, are distinctly Ojibwe or Odawa.[1] This means that the Bodwéwadmimwen Pokagon speaks varies from the best-documented uses of the language, from speakers in Wisconsin.[2] Those speakers' language use, conventions, and construction vary from the Bodwéwadmimwen spoken around Pokagon's villages. As mentioned earlier, there may be slight phonological, lexical, morphological, and even semantic differences between the better documented Potawatomi and the Neshnabemwen Pokagon utilizes. This stems, at least in part, from different language contact with other Algonquian-language-speaking people by Wisconsin Potawatomi and by the Catholic Potawatomi of the St. Joseph River Valley (also now known as Pokagon Potawatomi, or us, we, our, me, my, I).

Regardless of the *proper* designation for the Indian language that Pokagon speaks, by using English as a frame and inserting Potawatomi words and phrases, it is clear that Pokagon understands the power and validity that English holds to frame our legends and genesis. This is clear in his frequent use of Potawatomi words and phrases in every piece here, except for his most famous, *The Red Man's Rebuke*, where he only uses Potawatomi words twice, once to refer to God and once to refer to the devil. This code-mixing purposefully sets up a context to validate our Indian language and ways of being in the English-speaking sphere. Though it is interesting to note that Pokagon shies away from using what could have been too much Neshnabemwen in *The Red Man's Rebuke*, he does get to code-mix on his own terms in his retelling of our stories in English; he appeals to the power that prose and education have to validate our language in the eyes of others.

Creating space for Indigenous languages in the academy is a driving force behind some linguist-community "collaborative" documentation efforts. Putting Indigenous, minority languages in writing is some of the most validating work linguists do for some communities. In fact, it is not uncommon for a language community to request that the language be documented in a dictionary, or another form of printed, legitimizing work. These concrete forms of scholarship provide a historical reference point to prove the language has always existed and is tied to a certain community in a particular landscape or waterscape. Those documents can be used not only as references for members of the community but also as ways to validate their existence as Indigenous peoples to the government. Yet, since *The Red Man's Rebuke* creates a point of entry into the academic canon for Potawatomi spoken and chosen by a Potawatomi person at the time, the power and validity of having our language in our own words of our own volition for our own political and liturgical means creates a different sort of archive than does language documentation work.

Documentation efforts of the time did not have the political reach that Pokagon's *The Red Man's Rebuke* did. The few written primary sources of the Potawatomi language prior to Pokagon's publications were not collected by Native speakers of Potawatomi, or even Anishinaabemowin speakers living in Potawatomi linguistic, ethnic, or political communities. More than anything else as linguists and as Neshnabé peoples, we get to see Potawatomi language by way of our Francophone or Anglophone interlocutors, who were usually missionaries. For example, Father Gailland, though intensely devoted to documenting Potawatomi lexicon and grammar, did not have the same linguistic ideology or cultural grounding as Potawatomi people did and do.[3] A mismatch between community language ideology and researcher language ideology can have upsetting consequences, even when research is conducted in more attentive ways; the thoughts still come from outside institutions and disciplines. These collaborations may result in Indigenous community members noting that the relationships' boundaries may only be set and tested by the researcher and understood through Western frameworks.[4] The different views between researcher and researched are apparent when comparing the data in Gailland's dictionary to the Forest County Potawatomi Dictionary.[5] There are pleas for our language to fit into Gailland's framework seen in the translations he elicits: sabbath, salubrious, salary, savage, sanctimonious. The translation for "savage" according to Gailland is "Nīchinā'bê-k" or "pokōtch nīchinā'bê-k." These translations are actually the Father's spelling of "Neshnabék" (the plural form of Neshnabé), which for us literally means "the people." In other words, this is clearly a way to fit an endonym—Neshnabek, our word for ourselves—into the English concept of "savage." The exact circumstance of that unfortunate elicitation and translation are not apparent, but it is clear that to be Indian in Gailland's day was to be savage. For posterity's sake, Fr. Gailland's dictionary and grammatical sketches are helpful for language reclamation now, but they are not our own words; they are reinterpretations through an interlocutor. On the most basic level, it is unlikely that Gailland could accurately transcribe or understand the sounds he was hearing at the time since he wrote in his diary: "At first the sounds of the words appeared to me very strange and difficult, but by degrees, and as I commenced understanding it a little, it became daily easier and smoother to my mind, and I found it to my great astonishment a rich and expressive though uncultivated language."[6] He had neither a standardized orthography nor Native speaker intuitions to base his spellings or grammatical descriptions on.

The next archived language material we have access to as Potawatomi people comes out of Hockett's work on Potawatomi in the mid-twentieth century.[7] The documentary work Hockett gives the linguistic community cemented him as a good linguist, and it gave later linguists data to pull from. The Potawatomi data from speakers in Wisconsin (who came from Kansas) led the field to reexamine the way we think of morphology. Data from Potawatomi, English, and Georgian proved to be the most illustrative of the ways that morphological analysis failed to elegantly capture the generalizations of grammars, thus leading to the advent of a new morphological framework of analysis: distributed morphology.[8] Though Hockett's work has proven foundational, it is not for us. More recent scholars have collaborated in and with our Potawatomi communities to produce materials and grammars to be used on our own language reclamation journeys.[9] Indeed, we even have Potawatomi linguists now publishing work to give us a greater understanding of Potawatomi grammar in the linguistics canon, correcting earlier mistakes in the literature as well.[10]

As a result of language shift and endangerment, familial ties to language reclamation, interest in linguistics as a field of study, and a lot of good luck that I chose this family, body, and mind, I am allowed access to understanding not just Hockett's archive, but also Gailland's and Pokagon's. I am fortuitously situated as to understand a number of epistemologies and analytical frameworks. On that note, however, I would like to move away from the archives and field notes of others and bring our attention back to what Pokagon did for us. At the time, he took what he understood as the language and pressed it into print, forcing Americans to look at us on our land—from Chicago to South Haven and Paw Paw[11]—and forcing them to see us as Indigenous peoples still existing in our homelands by reading our words on our paper (birch bark). Now, we get to look at his representation of language and worldview, and we have to honor what it tells us about our historical and linguistic past, with a future-oriented framework. Though there is very little grammatical data in his writing, it is still important to see our people's ways of speaking written out.

An additional line of inquiry here comes from the sociolinguistic variation in Potawatomi communities of the late nineteenth century. Interestingly, first-wave sociolinguists of the mid-twentieth century posited that different groups of people, usually middle-class women, are the innovators of linguistic change and variation. On that note, it should be unsurprising that Pokagon was not a speaker of the Potawatomi we know existed in the late nineteenth century (based on the archive created by missionaries) since he heard his own parents speaking a different language or dialect that is not predicted to have been spoken in Pokagon's lands.

The power of Pokagon's writing leads to his naming as the "Red Man's Longfellow"—a pseudo-anachronistic philosopher, aiming for reparations, retribution, rematriation, and recognition on Chicago soil. I live in Hyde Park, Chicago, less than a mile from Jackson Park, home to the Columbian Exposition of 1893's grounds, home of the Obama Presidential Center (to push communities out lest community organizers push *them* out, or at least sign a community benefits agreement). The recognition Pokagon pleads for is still floating out of our collective grasp. At first, it is an acknowledgment of what was: "nokmeskignan" or "our grandmother earth" (exclusive first-person plural possession, ours but not yours). It is, in essence, our land. Later, it is a look into what it was: a well-to-do White neighborhood, equipped with its very own L-Train and bountiful green spaces; the perfect place to honor all that the "New World" has given European immigrants and their American descendants. Building a prop city for the World's Fair, not unlike the climax of *Blazing Saddles*. Now, it is a glance into what it had become: the Black Belt expanded to places such as Woodlawn and Jackson Park, no longer fully equipped with an L-Train; the South Side as a racist dog whistle rather than any mention of disinvestment, redlining, state-sanctioned violence, and expulsion. Soon, a neighborhood of the Presidential Center, a city unto its own for the transient population of university students, there by the grace of god or the devil to force Black residents out in a cyclic nature spurred ever on by the University of Chicago. What results is a disquieting feeling about time, coloniality, and gentrification. It is the cyclic displacements of Black and Indigenous people under the guise of ever-expanding borders and delineations of whiteness. Yet, this land is our land, but by no means does that entail our rebukes as the *Red Man* is heard.

Notes

1. Robert Eugene Lewis, "Potawatomi Discourse Markers" (PhD diss., University of Chicago).
2. C. Hockett (1937), Hockett Potawatomi Field Notebooks I, II, and III, in Laura Buszard-Welcher Papers on the Potawatomi Language, California Language Archives, University of California, Berkeley.
3. Rev. Maurice Gailland, SJ (1868), *Grammaire de la Langue Potêvatémie*, in Laura Buszard-Welcher Papers on the Potawatomi Language, Survey of California and Other Indian Languages, University of California, Berkeley; Rev. Maurice Gailland, SJ (n.d.), *A Complete English-Pottawatomie Dictionary*, Jesuit Missouri Province Archives, Reel no. 47, Jesuit Catalog no. NA 16.
4. Wesley Y. Leonard, "Centering Indigenous Ways of Knowing in Collaborative Language Work," in *Sustaining Indigenous Languages: Connecting Communities, Teachers, and Scholars* (Flagstaff: Northern Arizona University, 2021), 21–34. Also see Lenore A. Grenoble, "Linguistic Cages and the Limits of Linguists," in *Indigenous Language Revitalization: Encouragement, Guidance, and Lessons Learned*, ed. Jon Reyhner and Louise Lockard (Flagstaff: Northern Arizona University, 2009); Mary Hermes, Megan Bang, and Ananda Marin, "Designing Indigenous Language Revitalization," *Harvard Educational Review* 82, no. 3 (September 10, 2012): 381–402; and Wesley Y. Leonard, *Reflections on (De)colonialism in Language Documentation* (Honolulu: University of Hawai'i Press, 2018) for the history of colonial documentation of Indigenous languages.
5. Forest County Potawatomi Community, *Ézhe-bmadzimgek gdebodwéwadmi-zheshmomenan: Potawatomi Dictionary* (Crandon, WI: Forest County Potawatomi Community, 2014).
6. Maurice Gailland, "Early Years at St. Mary's Pottawatomie Mission: From the Diary of Father Maurice Gailland, SJ," ed. Rev. James M. Burke, *SJ Kansas Historical Quarterly* 20 (1953): 501–29.
7. Charles Hockett, "Potawatomi Syntax," *Language* 15, no. 4 (1939): 235–48; Charles Francis Hockett, *The Position of Potawatomi in Central Algonkian* (Michigan Academy of Science, Arts, and Letters, 1942); Charles F. Hockett, "Potawatomi I: Phonemics, Morphophonemics, and Morphological Survey," *International Journal of American Linguistics* 14, no. 1 (January 1948): 1–10; Charles F. Hockett, "Potawatomi II: Derivation, Personal Prefixes, and Nouns," *International Journal of American Linguistics* 14, no. 2 (April 1948): 63–73; Charles F. Hockett, "Potawatomi III: The Verb Complex," *International Journal of American Linguistics*, no. 3 (n.d.): 11; Charles F. Hockett, "Potawatomi IV: Particles and Sample Texts," *International Journal of American Linguistics* 14, no. 4 (October 1948): 213–25; Charles F. Hockett, "What Algonquian Is Really Like," *International Journal of American Linguistics* 32, no. 1 (January 1966): 59–73.
8. Morris Halle and Alec Marantz, "Some Key Features of Distributed Morphology," *MIT Working Papers in Linguistics* 21 (1994): 275–88.
9. Laura Ann Buszard, "Constructional Polysemy and Mental Spaces in Potawatomi Discourse" (PhD diss., University of California, Berkeley).
10. Robert Eugene Lewis Jr., "Potawatomi Discourse Markers" (PhD diss., University of Chicago, 2020).
11. Paw Paw is named after a fruit tree whose scientific name *triloba asimina* comes from our word for pawpaws: *asimnen*, possibly from another Algonquian language, but certainly a cognate form.

Summary for *Pottawatamie Book of Genesis*

Blaire Morseau

As the title suggests, this story recounts the creation of the first man and woman by ktthémnedo or the Great Spirit. If updated to today's orthography, the title would read *Dbathmowen Bodéwadmi é wzhetowen Neshnabé*; however, as Malott points out, this phrasing is very English-oriented. "The verb structure simply doesn't work that way in the Potawatomi language." A more accurate Bodwéwadmimwen phrase might be: *Neshnabé égi gzhémayét dbathmowen* or "the story of when the Neshnabé was created." The story itself begins with a storm. Upon summoning lightning at the shores of a beautiful lake, the Great Spirit molds the pair from red clay. Some of the lesser spirits retreat from fear and jealousy of the beautiful creation and intend to cause misfortune to humans in hunting and in war. As a result, Neshnabék will sometimes attempt to appease bad spirits with food and gifts, or they may bring with them an animal for protection—otherwise known as their clan relative. These might be symbols of bears, otters, sturgeon, and many more. Pokagon explains that a custom among Native peoples in the Great Lakes

33

region is to name children after animals whom they resemble. This, he explains, is the origin of the patrilineal clan system that tribes still use today. He explains as a concluding remark that while this custom may seem silly, these stories and these ways of living are "as sacred to us" as those of the White race.

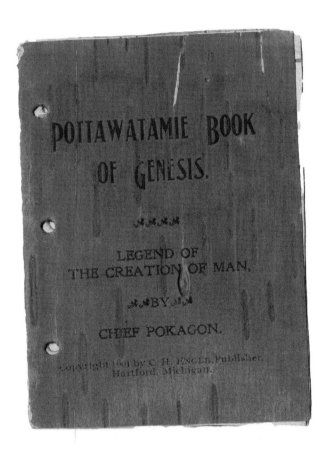

FIGURE 2. Book cover of *Pottawatamie Book of Genesis*, Center for History and Culture, Pokagon Band, Dowagiac, 2018.8.14, 1901.

Dibangimowin Pottawattamie Ejitodwin Aunishnawbe

(Pottawattamie Legend of the Creation of Man)

Chief Pokagon

There is an old tradition among our people dimly seen through the mists of time, that Ki-ji Man-i-to (The Great Spirit),[1] after he had created nomash (the fish)[2] of ni-bi-nong (the waters),[3] and b-nes-sig (the fowls)[4] of no-din (the air),[5] and mo-naw-to-auk (the beasts)[6] of a-ki (the land).[7] His work still failed to satisfy the grand conception of His soul. Hence He called a great Council of man-i-to-og (the spirits)[8] that ruled over land and seas, His agents, and revealed unto them how it was the great desire of Nin o-daw (His heart)[9] to create a new being that should stand erect upon his hind legs, and to possess the combined intelligence of all the living creatures He had made.

Most of those spirits whom He had permitted to hold dominion over the earth, when they met in the grand Council, encouraged His Divine plans, but Man-i-to O-gi-maw-og (the spiritual Chiefs)[10] when they considered the great power the proposed being might wield, quietly withdrew themselves from the Council, and held a private pow wow of their own, to frustrate, if possible, the plans of How-waw-tuck (the Almighty).[11] The loyal Mon-i-tog who remained at the grand Council stood aghast as Ki-ji Man-i-to revealed unto them His Divine plan, explaining the great possibilities that awaited the new creature He had conceived in His heart to create.

The Divine Council was prolonged by debate from the set of sun until morning dawn. Ke-sus (the sun)[12] arose in greater brilliancy than ever before. The Spirits anxiously began to inquire of His Majesty, "How many suns and moons would pass before He could accomplish His wonderful work?" While yet the inquiry hung on ki o-don-og (their lips),[13] He said unto them: "Follow me." He led them into a great wilderness to Sa-gi-i-gan,[14] a beautiful inland lake. And as He stood upon the shores thereof in the presence of them all, His eyes flashed wa-saw mo-win (lightning)![15] The lake became boiling water! The earth trembled! He then spake in a voice of thunder: "COME FORTH YE LORDS OF AU-KEE (the world)!"[16] The ground opened! And from out of the red clay that lined the lake came forth Au-ne-ne gaie Ik-we (man and woman)[17] like kego (flying fish) from out the water! In presence of the new born pair, all was still as death! A dark cloud hung over the lake! It began to boil again. The awful silence was then broken! The earth shook! And Ki-ji Man-ito said: "Come forth ye servants of Au-nish-naw-be (man)!"[18] Forth leaped at once from out the lake Ni-ji wa-be gon o-nim-og (a pair of snow-white dogs)[19] and laid down where stood the new made pair kissing their feet and hands.

The bride and groom then each other fondly kissed as hand in hand they stood, in naked innocence, in the full bloom of youth, perfect in make and mould, of body and of limb. Ki-gi-nos maw-kaw mis-taw-kaw (their long black hair)[20] almost reached the ground, which, gently waving in nip-nong oden (the morning breeze)[21] in contrast with their rich color, grace, and forms erect, outrivaled in beauty all other creatures He had made. They looked all about them in wonder and surprise. Surveyed all living creatures that moved in sight. Gazed upon the towering trees. The grass. The flowers. The lake. The sun shine and the shade. And again at each other fondly kissed, as their eyes looked love to eyes, with no other language their feelings to express.

At length I-kwe (the maiden fair)[22] slily let go Os-ki-nawe o-ning-i-maw (the young man's hand)[23] and stole away into the dark shades and hid, where she might watch to test his love, and learn thereby if his feelings were akin to her's [*sic*]. Long he sought in vain to find his mate, until at length the snow-white dogs, following on her track, joyfully howled out: "We have found her."

Now when mau-tchi Man-i-tog (the spiritual Chiefs) first learned that Ki-ji Man-i-to had finished His crowning works, as He had proposed to do, sought diligently for the new made pair until they found them. And as they surveyed the beauty of their forms erect, and the surpassing loveliness of body and limb, their wonder and admiration was unbounded. But when they saw the soul of the Divine shining in their faces, like the noon-day sun, their hearts were stung through and through by maw-tchi a-mog (the cruel wasps)[24] of envy and jealousy. Hence they resolved, in nin o-daw (their hearts), that instead of trying to live in peace with them, as they had done with the first creation, they would do all they could to make them discontented, unhappy and miserable.

As time rolled on, our first o-nig-go-maw (parents)[25] and generations after them, began to realize there were mau-tchi dash meno Mandito (bad spirits and good spirits)[26] that exercised dominion over mountains, lakes, streams and plains, and that they were in a measure controlled by them. They also began to learn that au-nish-i-naw-be (man) possessed the nature and the intelligence of all the animal creation; and that he was endowed with a spiritual nature which was given him by mi-si ge-go ga-gi-ji-tod (the Creator of all things)[27] in waw-kwing dash Au-kee (in heaven and on earth).[28] Hence when they were unfortunate in securing game, or unsuccessful in battle, it was all attributed to the bad spirits that held dominion over the country wherein they dwelt.

And when game was plenty, and they were successful in battle, this they attributed to the good spirits that controlled the land in which they lived. Sometimes in order to appease bad spirits, they made offerings of fruits and grains. But they sacrificed animals only to Ki-ji Man-i-to waw-quin [the God of Heaven] who alone they recognized as the great Creator and Ruler of all things in heaven and on earth.

Our fathers and mothers in their primeval state, did not name their children as do the civilized races, simply that they might be known and designated by them. But when their children were born, whatever animal or bird they imagined they most resembled they were called by that name; and as strange as it may appear to the whole white race, in after generations those bearing the name of some animal believed, at least they claimed, to have descended from such animal whose name they bore. It might be maw-qua [the bear],[29] or waw-goosh [the fox],[30] or mi-gi-si [the eagle].[31] The same rule followed in each individual case. And so it was in succeeding generations, each tribe or clan adopted as their "to-tum"[32] the animal or thing whose name the patriarch of the tribe was called when a child.

Sometimes when at war, the animal was taken with them alive, but generally it was painted on a tanned hide and used as white men use their flags.

It was an emblem of royalty as well as a symbol of loyalty, and when engaged in battle a warrior would rather die than surrender his totum.

It matters not how foolish our legends may appear to those races who call themselves civilized, still they were as sacred to us as holy writ to them.

Notes

"*Dibangimowin Pottawattamie Ejitodwin Aunishnawbe* (Pottawattamie Legend of the Creation of Man)" was the original spelling and translation offered by Pokagon. Advanced language specialist and contributor to this collection, Kyle Malott offers *Neshnabé ėgi gzhémayét dbathmowen* as an updated and more accurate translation for the title of this story. *Neshnabé ėgi gzhémayét dbathmowen* translates to "the story of when the Neshnabé was created."

1. *Ki-ji Man-i-to* is now spelled *Ktthėmnedo* or *Gzhémnedo*.
2. *Nomash* could possibly be *names* for "little sturgeon."
3. *Ni-bi-nong* is now spelled *mbinak* and translates to "place of waters."
4. *B-nes-sig* is now spelled *bnéshik* and translates to "birds."
5. *No-din* is now spelled *noden* and translates to "wind."
6. *Mo-naw-to-auk* is now spelled *mnedowêk* and translates to "spirits." If referring to animals or beasts one would use *wésiyêk*.
7. *A-ki* is now spelled *kė* and translates to "land." *Aki* is most commonly used in Ojibwe.
8. *Man-i-to-og* is now spelled *mnedok*.
9. *Nin o-daw* translates to "his or her heart" and should be spelled *wdé'*. Pokagon seems to have used a variation of *nin* and *wdé*, which mean "I" and "heart," respectively.
10. *Man-i-to O-gi-maw-og* is now spelled *mnedo wgemak* and translates to "the chief of spirits."
11. It is unclear where the word *How-waw-tuck* comes from; it does not exist within Potawatomi, Odawa, or Ojibwe. It is possible that this word may be Mascouten. If referring to the Creator, you would hear *Gzhémnedo*, *Ktthėmnedo*, or *Mamwëgosnan*.
12. *Ke-sus* is now spelled *gizes* and translates to "he or she is rising," referring to the sun or moon.
13. A reference for *ki o-don-og* could not be found in any of the three languages. *Wdonwan* would be used for "their lips."
14. *Zagen* or "lake." *Sa-gi-i-gan* is a word primarily used in Odawa and Ojibwe, but is very rarely seen in Potawatomi. One will mostly see *mbes*.
15. *Wa-saw mo-win* is now spelled *wawasmowen* and translates to "lightning." In Potawatomi one will also see *wawasmok* or *wawasmëwêk*.
16. *Au-kee* is now spelled *kė* and translates to "land." In Potawatomi the Earth is usually referred to as *gokmeskinan* or "our grandmother Earth."
17. *Au-ne-ne gaie Ik-we* is now spelled *néné minė kwé* and translates to "man and woman."

Pokagon's use is specifically in Ojibwe; Potawatomi doesn't use "gaie."

18. *Au-nish-naw-be* is now spelled *Neshnabé* and refers to a "Native American person." The strong "au" sound at the beginning of the word can be attributed to Odawa and Ojibwe.

19. *Ni-ji wa-be gon o-nim-og* is now spelled *nish wabnëmêk* and translates to "two white dogs."

20. *Ki-gi-nos maw-kaw mis-taw-kaw* is *Gnëmkedéwankwéwêk* and translates to "they have long black hair." Pokagon's language use is very broken here.

21. *Nip-nong oden* is now spelled *nib noden* and translates to "summer wind."

22. *I-kwe* is now spelled *kwé* and translates to "woman." This is an example of a romanticized translation in Pokagon's texts.

23. *Os-ki-nawe o-ning-i-maw* is now spelled *shkenwé wnetth* and translates to "the young man's hand."

24. *Maw-tchi a-mog* is now spelled *mthe'amok* and translates to "the bad wasps."

25. *O-nig-go-maw* is now spelled *wgetsimen* and translates to "his or her parents." Here Pokagon uses an Ojibwe word to describe his/her parents.

26. *Mau-tchi dash meno Mandito* is now spelled *mthemnedok minė mnomnedok*. Again you can see the Ojibwe influence with the word "dash," which is not used in Potawatomi.

27. *Mi-si ge-go ga-gi-ji-tod* is now spelled *thak gégo ga gishtot* and translates to "the one who created everything." The "mi-si" (*méz-*) particle used describes being all over the place.

28. *Waw-kwing dash Au-kee* is now spelled *wawkwik minė kik* and translates to "heaven and earth."

29. *Maw-qua* is now spelled *mko* and translates to "bear." The Ojibwe word for bear is *makwa*.

30. *Waw-goosh* is now spelled *wagosh* and translates to "fox."

31. *Mi-gi-si* is now spelled *mgezhwash* and translates to "bald eagle." The Ojibwe use *migizi* for bald eagle.

32. *To-tum* is now spelled *wdodémen* and translates to "his or her clan." Pokagon uses the word without the possessive marks that are required on this word.

Summary and Geological Context for
Algonquin Legends of Paw Paw Lake

Nicholas Marcelletti and Blaire Morseau

I n this birch bark book, Simon Pokagon shares a story passed down to him and his tribe from an "ancient" group of Neshnabé peoples who lived in the area currently known as southwest Michigan. He describes a great bay where the present-day Paw Paw Lake was at the extreme western edge. He explains that the shoreline extended north to Bangor, Michigan, south to Hartford, Michigan, and finally westward at the length of a "canoe's day journey." Lastly, Pokagon further illustrates this watershed by mentioning that the current bodies of water—Rush Lake and Van Auken Lake—used to be part of this great bay. To further aid in visualizing this ancient landscape, figure 3 uses Pokagon's descriptions to map the approximate location of this great bay.

As a young geology student several decades ago, Nicholas Marcelletti and his professors agreed that Pokagon's story sounded like a very accurate description of the failure of a natural lake embankment, the resulting flood, and the flood aftereffects. If one looks at the videos of the 2020 failure of Edenville Earthen Dam in Gladwin County, Michigan, for instance, and the resulting flood as Wixom Lake drained away, one would note many similarities to Pokagon's description. Therefore, it appears his story is based on an actual historical event, lending further credence to the validity of oral history and traditional forms of

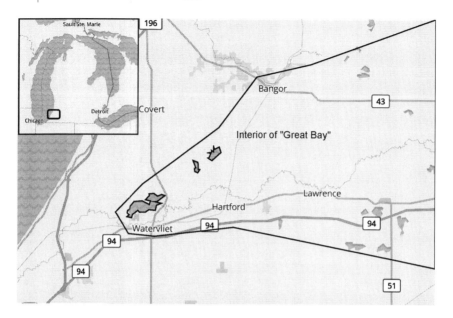

FIGURE 3. Map of southwest Michigan with plot points near Bangor and Hartford connected by a curved line showing the approximate location of the ancient bay's western shoreline. The locations of present-day Paw Paw Lake, Rush Lake, and Van Auken Lake are also outlined. Created by Blaire Morseau, 2022.

storytelling that have often been dismissed as unreliable folklore by non-Native historians, archaeologists, and many others.

Geologists have a name for the type of flood described in Pokagon's story—a "glacial outburst flood." This type of flood, which is very common in the Himalayas, occurs when a bank moraine or a line of hills formed by glacial deposits fails, releasing the glacial lake's waters. Further evidence that Pokagon's description is based on an actual historical event relates to both the time of year in which the glacial outburst flood occurred as well as the reactions of the dogs that Pokagon describes. Pokagon mentions that the flood occurred in the spring. This is significant, because spring rains could have saturated the natural embankment that contained the lake, causing it to fail. Second, on the way to investigate the source of the noise, the dogs accompanying the men, women, and children whine and cringe as they never had done before. There are numerous documented accounts of dogs responding to seismic events by howling. But what of the contemporary visual evidence of such a large, ancient bay? What sort of topographical evidence is there for the immense body of water that Pokagon describes as existing in antiquity?

Today, with the aid of Google Earth and with a trained eye (or perhaps even an untrained eye), one can easily identify three possible locations for Simon Pokagon's Lake: The first is located directly north of Paw Paw in Van Buren County, Michigan, along the main branch of the Paw Paw River. This relatively small river only occupies the middle of this valley. However, this valley at its widest point is approximately 3.70 miles wide (or approximately 6 kilometers). This valley abruptly comes to an end just east of the intersection of 44th Avenue and 46th Street (near the border between Paw Paw and Waverly Townships in Van Buren County, Michigan). The geomorphological feature that is interesting about this valley is the valley containing the Paw Paw River channel, as it is significantly wider in comparison to the modern river. The average width of this valley is approximately 2.48 miles or 4 kilometers wide, while the average width of the Paw Paw River channel is only 50–70 feet wide (approximately 17 meters). This discrepancy in size leads to the assertion that the stream is underfit for the channel. The surface sediments in this valley are mostly comprised of sand, silt, and clay. In geology silts and clays are indicators for a lacustrine origin of the sediments (lake deposits) as opposed to coarse sands and gravels. The larger sediment size is indicative of faster-moving water or streams, while the finer sediments—silts and clays—indicate still water, a lacustrine lake environment.

The second possible location starts southwest of Lawton, Michigan, and trends in a southwesterly direction past the south end of Decatur, Michigan, before this well-defined valley disappears in the northwest of Dowagiac, Michigan. This valley is unique in that it is drained by two different rivers flowing in different directions. The north end of this valley is drained by the South Branch of the Paw Paw River, which flows in a northerly direction. The south end of this valley is drained by the Dowagiac Drain, which flows in a southwesterly direction. The divide between the two drainage basins appears to be located near the intersection of 39th Street and 82nd Avenue in Decatur Township. This is another example of a river valley where the valley is significantly wider than the river channel. In this case the valley averages approximately 1.5 miles in width (2.4 kilometers), while the South Branch of the Paw Paw River and/or Dowagiac Drain are both approximately 20 to 30 feet wide (approximately 7.7 meters). The surface sediments in this valley are peat, marl (a freshwater clay sediment), silts, and fine sands. Once again, these types of sediments indicate a lacustrine (lake depositional) environment. Finally, previous studies have identified at least part of this area as "Glacial Lake Dowagiac."[1]

The third location is much smaller than the first two and is located along the East Branch of the Paw Paw River. It is best visible just to the east of where County Road 653 crosses I-94 in Antwerp Township, in Van Buren County, Michigan. In the 1890s a large portion of this area was flooded to form a mill-pond.[2] The dam for this millpond was located near the eastern village limits of Paw Paw, Michigan. From the dam this millpond extended east past where the East Branch of the Paw Paw River crosses County Road 653. This valley averages between 800 to 1,500 feet in width, while the average width of the East Branch of the Paw Paw River is approximately 6 to 8 feet (1.83 to 2.43 meters). In addition, Mud Lake and Sand Lake are located adjacent to this valley and could possibly be remnants of Simon Pokagon's Lake. All three of these locations in Van Buren County could have all been connected at one time to make one large single body of water. Present-day wetlands maps show evidence of this, as represented in figure 4.

Physical evidence would consist of actual physical features left over from the flood and/or features that could clearly be identified as lacustrine in origin. However, to identify these physical features we would have to have either a geological or geomorphology study that identified such features. Figure 4 is a review of the applicable studies in the area that Marcelletti has been able to identify to date.

No geological study in the area to date has provided solid evidence of Simon's Lake. However, there have been some studies that come tangibly close. The second location in this article was identified as "Glacial Lake Dowagiac."[3] However, in 1955 Terwilliger identified the region shown in figures 3 and 4 as "glacial drainage ways," or channels of fast-moving glacial meltwater. Yet, when one reviews the evidence, lake bodies have little or no movement of water other than seasonal temperature inversions. Only bayous—defined as slow-moving streams with poorly defined margins—are similar to the lakes described here. So, if Terwilliger was correct and these areas are glacial drainage ways, then the sediments in all three valleys would be comprised predominantly of peats, silts, and clays (at least near surface materials) as these types of sediments indicate a lacustrine depositional "lake environment," not a fast-moving water as described by Terwilliger's report.[4] The Cummings, Twenter, and Holtschlag (1984) report identified the land use and the elevations of the moraines in the

Wetlands Map Viewer

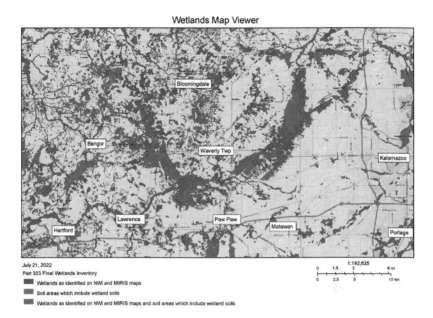

July 21, 2022
Part 303 Final Wetlands Inventory

▨ Wetlands as identified on NWI and MIRIS maps
▨ Soil areas which include wetland soils
▨ Wetlands as identified on NWI and MIRIS maps and soil areas which include wetland soils

1:192,625

0 1.5 3 6 mi
0 2.5 5 10 km

FIGURE 4. Wetland map of southwest Michigan with Hartford Township in the lower left, Bangor in the middle-left, and Paw Paw in the lower-middle of the image. Sources: Esri, HERE, Garmin, USGS, Intermap, INCREMENT P, NRCan, Esri Japan, METI, Esri China (Hong Kong), Esri Korea, Esri (Thailand), NGCC, (c) OpenStreetMap contributors, and the GIS User Community. Map generated by Nicholas Marcelletti, 2022.

county and surficial flow and did not look at the geologic process that created the various landforms in Van Buren County.[5]

Finally, Bird (2005) studied a limited area in Van Buren County, investing only three of its United States Geological Survey (USGS) quadrangles in Decatur, Lawrence, and Paw Paw, Michigan.[6] The primary purpose of his study was to examine the surficial sediments that are exposed at the surface or immediately below the soil horizon in the area. A secondary purpose of the study was to characterize the buried sediments. For subsurface deposits the lithology along with the relative stratigraphic sequence was examined. The relationship expressed between the sediment assemblages and the juxtaposition with topography was also investigated. This, along with the sequence stratigraphy, can be used to re-create a picture of glacial-related events that shaped the landscape of these three quadrangles. Bird concluded that at one time three areas mentioned earlier were part of a proto-glacial lake. This conclusion was further verified by the identification of sediments that were deposited as a result of a lacustrine environment.

Geological studies in Van Buren have provided some evidence to verify that a great lake that Pokagon mentions in *Legends of Paw Paw Lake* did exist after the final retreat of the glaciers from the area. However, these geological studies have failed to identify any evidence of a breach of the banks of this historical lake and the resulting catastrophic flood. The evidence for such a flood may yet be found. Such a deposit could consist of large boulders, since these are indicative of episodic flood events (which result when an embankment or ice dam fails). As stated earlier, the deposits from these floods contain large boulders and cobbles that are usually structureless and are diffusely stratified. These types of characteristics of depositional units are interpreted as the result of sudden, rapid flow, followed by rapid deposition. Additional evidence could also be obtained in the carbon 14 dating of organic material that would be found buried in the sediments suspected of having been flood-deposited. Finally, the archeological evidence would be a Native American village located on an area that would have once been on the shores of this historical lake, with carbon dating of any fish remains found in the area of these settlements.

While Marcelletti is trained as a geologist and not as an archaeologist, he has reviewed several archeological studies for this area. There are several interesting finds that point to the fact that the "ancient" people that inhabited this area "pre-contact" (with Europeans) had a diet that consisted extensively of fish. This is based on excavations performed at pre-contact settlements that identified extensive remains of various great lake fishes of the area. So, it would make sense to have Pokagon's settlement located next to a source of these fish. Finally, waterways in the pre-contact time period provided the fastest and most efficient method of transportation. Thus, it would seem sensible to have these settlements near bodies of water that could provide access to wide areas. In addition to geological studies that would verify Pokagon's story, the authors would also like to see archeological studies that could identify a settlement location adjacent to one of the three locations identified in this essay.

Notes

1. Frank Leverett and Frank Bursley Taylor, *The Pleistocene of Indiana and Michigan and the History of the Great Lakes* (Washington, DC: U.S. Government Printing Office, 1915).
2. See late 1800s Historical Atlas, Van Buren County, Michigan.
3. I. C. Russell and Frank Leverett, "Description of the Ann Arbor Quadrangle," USGS Archeological Atlas Survey 155 (Washington, DC: U.S. Geological Survey, 1915), 15.
4. T. R. Cummings, F. R. Twenter, and D. J. Holtschlag, "Hydrology and Land Use in Van Buren County, Michigan, Water Resources Investigation Report 84-4112, prepared in cooperation with Van Buren County, Michigan Department of Natural Resources, Michigan Department of Agriculture U.S. Geological Survey," 1984.
5. F. W. Terwilliger, "The Glacial Geology and Groundwater Resources of Van Buren County, Michigan," Occasional Papers for 1954 Michigan State Geological Survey, 1954, p. 95.
6. Brian Bird, "Glacial Stratigraphy and Surficial Geology of the Decatur, Lawrence, and Paw Paw U.S.G.S.7.5 Minute Quadrangles in Van Buren County, Michigan" (master's thesis, Western Michigan University, 2005).

FIGURE 5. Book cover of *Algonquin Legends of Paw Paw Lake*, Center for History and Culture, Pokagon Band, Dowagiac, 2018.8.10, 1901.

Algonquin Legends of Paw Paw Lake

Chief Pokagon

No more for us the wild deer bounds;
The plow is on our hunting grounds.

Many, many bi-bon-og nin-go-twak (hundred years ago)[1] tradition as sacred to us as Holy Writ to the white man, tells us that Paw Paw Lake was a bay at the extreme western limit of sa-gi-a-gan (a great inland lake)[2] called by ancient Au-nish-a-naw-beg (the Indians)[3] Ki-tchi-git-a-gan[4] meaning an earthly Paradise.

This great lake filled the valley of the Paw Paw river a canoe day's journey towards the rising sun; and further they tell us it extended from the foot hills just south of the present site of Hartford village to the foot hills just north of where Bangor village is now located.

At that time An-a-kan (Rush lake)[5] and Wawbi-gan (Swan lake)[6] now called Van Auken lake, were bays connected with this large body of water on the north.

One of the largest o-de-na-wan (Indian villages)[7] then known was built around this bay on the side towards the setting sun.

This village was called Waw-kwin (Heaven),[8] a happy hunting ground. Near by it was A-ki Ga-besh-i-win (a tribal camping ground).[9] The great mi-kan (trail)[10] of all the northern and western tribes passed this place to and from mas-ko-de (the great prairie)[11] beyond Lake Michigan.

It was indeed an important place. Mo-o-se (elk),[12] pi-gi-ka (buffalo),[13] maw-qui (bear)[14] and suc-se (deer)[15] in their autumn and spring migrations, either north or south, passed around the western limit of this great body of water; while unnumbered millions of me-me-og (wild pigeons)[16] in early spring time filled all the trees in the big forest with their nests, extending west to Lake Michigan and northward sometimes beyond Maw-kaw-te (Black river).[17]

This wonderful lake swarmed with gi-go (fish)[18] and shi-seb, ni-kag and waw-bi si- (ducks, geese and swan)[19] floated in clouds upon its waters. In fact this ancient tribe lived in such luxury and ease that the chase was abandoned, for they could procure all bi-nes-si, we-i-was and gi-go (fowl, flesh and fish)[20] they wanted to eat in bi-no-dan (near bow shot)[21] of their wigwams. While this favored tribe was living in the lap of ease and luxury, one night in early spring, they were aroused from their slumbers at midnight by a strange roaring sound, such as they had never heard before.

At first, they thought it might be an-i-mi-ka (thunder)[22] but as no waw-so-mo-win (lightning)[23] flashed across the sky they concluded it must be an on-coming wan-a-ton (cyclone),[24] yet that did not seem possible as not an-a-kwad (a cloud)[25] was anywhere to be seen. Finally they started in the direction of the strange roaring sound, men, women and children, followed by a multitude of o-nin-og (dogs)[26] whining and cringing as they had never done before.

Moving cautiously southward they finally reached the headlands north of where the village of Watervliet now stands, and gazing into the valley beneath, they saw by the feeble light of the moon that the shore at the outlet of their beautiful lake which for ages had held it fast, had given way and a deluge of water, roaring like a whirlwind, was sweeping down great trees and rocks towards Lake Michigan.

When morning came they beheld where Lake Sa-gi-a-gan lay when the sun went down, like an infant sleeping in its mother's arms, a dark roily stream which appeared like some monstrous snake pushing its way through slime and mud, boiling on either side with struggling fish. Turning from the revolting sight with saddened hearts, they returned to their village. Here they found to their surprise the bay had receded a bow's shot from their canoes, that lay the night before in circles around the shore, and their beautiful wik-wad (bay)[27] was changed into a lake as it now appears.

Coming to a more recent date, when our tribe the Pottawattamies took possession of southern Michigan, it may be interesting to know that we called

Paw Paw Lake Sa-bi-na go-na, meaning "It swallows the river in storm and spews it out in sunshine."[28] This name was given because in wet weather the river runs into the outlet of the lake and in a dry time it runs out at the same place into the river again. Hence the name from the Algonquin words meaning swallow and vomit. Indians in naming their children always give some reason for the name, and in naming places the same custom is adhered to.

Pokagon does not wish to complain of the white man, yet must admit he longs, in his heart, again to behold the beauty of Si-bi-naw go-naw, the o-de-na of his fathers. Here we killed the bear, the elk and the deer. Here we trapped ni-kig, es-i-can and aw-mik (the otter, coon and beaver).[29] But alas, our forests have been cut down! Our woodland flowers, for want of shade, have faded and died! Our ancient trails cannot be traced! Our fathers graves have been destroyed, and where our wigwams once stood and our children played now stands the cottages of the white man. All, all has changed except gi-sis, tib-i-gisis and an-ang-og (the sun, moon and stars),[30] and they have not because their God and Ki-ji Man-i-to (our God)[31] in great wisdom and mercy, hung them beyond the white man's reach.

Notes

1. *Bi-bon-og nin-go-twak* is now spelled *ėgi ngotwak pongëk* and translates to "one hundred years ago."
2. *Sa-gi-a-gan* is now spelled *zagen* and translates to "lake." Pokagon's phrase is a word that is primarily used in Odawa and Ojibwe but is very rarely seen in Potawatomi.
3. *Au-nish-a-naw-beg* is now spelled *Neshnabék* and refers to a "Native American person." The strong "au" sound at the beginning of the word can be attributed to Odawa and Ojibwe. *Au-nish-naw-be* and *Neshnabé* are both singular forms of the noun. *Au-nish-a-naw-beg* and *Neshnabék* are both plural. The "g" in the first word and the "k" in the updated spelling of the word make the noun plural.
4. *Ki-tchi-git-a-gan* is now spelled *ktthė gtegan* and translates to "a big garden." This is an example of romanticized translations by Pokagon.
5. *An-a-kan* is now spelled *Nagneshkëmbes* and translates to "Rush Lake." The word for Rush Lake is *Nagneshkëmbes*, which translates as bulrush lake; *an-a-kan* (*nakën*) just means "a bulrush mat."
6. *Wawbi-gan* is now spelled *Wabzhi mbes* and translates to "Swan Lake." The word *wawbi-gan* (*wabgën*) actually means "clay."
7. *O-de-na-wan* is now spelled *odanwan* and translates to "their villages."
8. *Waw-kwin* is now spelled *wawkwik* and translates to "heaven."
9. *A-ki Ga-besh-i-win* is now spelled *gbéshénak* and translates to "a place used for camping."
10. *Mi-kan* is now spelled *mikan* and translates to "trail/path."

11. *Mas-ko-de* is now spelled *mshkodé* and translates to "prairie."
12. *Mo-o-se* is now spelled *mzhéwé* and translates to "elk." *Moz* or *mozo* is "moose."
13. *Pi-gi-ka* is now spelled *bzhêké* and translates to "buffalo."
14. *Maw-qui* is now spelled *mko* and translates to "bear."
15. *Suc-se* is now spelled *seksi* and translates to "deer."
16. *Me-me-og* is now spelled *mimiyêk* and translates to "pigeons."
17. *Maw-kaw-te* is now spelled *Mkedé zibé* and translates to "Black River."
18. *Gi-go* is now spelled *gigo* and translates to "fish."
19. *Shi-seb*, *ni-kag*, and *waw-bi si-* are now spelled *zhishib*, *nkëg*, and *wabzhi* and translate to "the duck, goose, and swan." Pokagon's Anishinaabe phrasing is plural, but the English language used was in the singular form.
20. *Bi-nes-si*, *we-i-was*, and *gi-go* are now spelled *bnéshi*, *wëyas*, and *gigo* and translate to "bird, meat, and fish."
21. *Bi-no-dan* is now spelled *bimodan* and translates to "he or she shoots something with a bow."
22. *An-i-mi-ka* is now spelled *nemki* and translates to "thunder being." "An-i-mi-ka" (nemki) is more used in Odawa and Ojibwe for a thunder being; Potawatomi will mostly use *thigwé*.
23. *Waw-so-mo-win* is now spelled *wawasmowen* and translates to "lightning."
24. *Wan-a-ton* is now spelled *wawyaten* and translates to "circular motion." It appears Pokagon was using the word "wawyaten," which is used to describe a circular motion as in a whirlpool or cyclone.
25. *An-a-kwad* is now spelled *ankwet* and translates to "cloud."
26. *O-nin-og* is now spelled *nëmoshêk* and translates to "dogs." "Nëm" is a shortened form of the more commonly heard "nëmoshêk."
27. *Wik-wad* is now spelled *kwikwiyak* and translates to "bay."
28. *Sa-bi-na go-na* is now spelled *zaginagwna* and translates to "he or she outwardly swallows someone." It should be noted that "someone" in Potawatomi does not necessarily mean a human, but any entity that is animate, such as certain stones, animals, plants, etc.
29. *Ni-kig*, *es-i-can*, and *aw-mik* are now spelled *gdedé*, *éspen*, and *mëk* and translate to "the otter, raccoon, and beaver." "Ni-kig" (*ngig*) and "aw-mik" (*amik*) are both used specifically in Ojibwe.
30. *Gi-sis*, *tib-i-gisis*, and *an-ang-og* are now spelled *gizes*, *dbëk gizes*, and *nëgosêk* and translate to "the sun, moon, and stars."
31. *Ki-ji Man-i-to* is now spelled *Ktthê mnedo* and translates to "Great Spirit." The term Pokagon uses does not have the possessive marker of "ours." Another word commonly used is *mamwëgosnan* or "our greatest father."

Summary for *Algonquin Legends of South Haven*

This story of South Haven, Michigan, is given to us from what Simon Pokagon refers to as an ancient tribe of Neshnabék called "Mash-ko-de" or Prairie people before they were driven out by the Odawas. The story recounts how Ktthėmnedo took his throne at the highest point between the Black River and Lake Michigan, where he contemplated his next creations. Spreading beautiful glistening stones, serenading songbirds, and woodland flowers across the land, he proceeded to make a giant bow that he placed on the shores of the lake. Perhaps it is no coincidence that along the eastern shores of Lake Michigan up to the northern Straits of Mackinac, and finally south along the western shores of Lake Huron one might interpret the water's shape as a bow—a bow "in the clouds without arrow, string or quiver." Ktthėmnedo, explains Pokagon, created this bow so that future generations will value peace and not war.

After sharing this ancient story, Pokagon describes how after the Potawatomis started living in the region of what is currently called South Haven, they named it "Nik-o-nong," or beautiful sunset. A bustling town,

53

Nik-o-nong was a crossroads of many tribes near and far on account of its proximity to waterways and footpaths. Pokagon concludes his story lamenting the loss of such beauty—wrought in no small part by the ecological destruction of American "progress."

FIGURE 6. Book cover of *Algonquin Legends of South Haven*, Center for History and Culture, Pokagon Band, Dowagiac, 2018.8.7, 1901.

Algonquin Legends of South Haven

Chief Pokagon

No more for us the wild deer bounds;
The plow is on our hunting grounds.

Our traditional account of South Haven given us by ki-os-ag (our forefathers)[1] was held as sacred by them as holy writ by white men. Long, long bi-bong (years)[2] ago Ki-ja-Man-i-to (the great spirit)[3] who held dominion over Mi-shi-gan (Lake Michigan)[4] and the surrounding country, selected Haw-waw-naw, a place at the o-don (mouth)[5] of Maw-kaw-te (Black River)[6] as his seat of government. His royal throne "Ki-tchi-wik"[7] was located on the highest point of that neck of land lying between Maw-kaw-te River and Lake Michigan. This high point of land was called Ish-pem-ing, meaning a high place. Here it was that Ki-ja-Man-i-to worked out the great conceptions of ki-tchi-tchang (his soul).[8] With giant strides he scattered broadcast along the shore, a day's journey northward, multitudes of beautiful stones of various color, shape and size, that in sunshine outshone tchi-be-kan-a (the galaxy on High).[9]

No such charming stones, excepting those, could anywhere be found around all the shores of the great lake.

He also planted in saw-kaw (the forests)[10] along the shore the most beautiful woodland flowers that ever bloomed on Earth; and filled all the trees with birds that sang the sweetest songs that ever fell on mortal ears. He also made a great mit-ig-wab (bow)[11] at least two arrow flights in length, and placed it along the shore. He then painted it from end to end in beautiful lines, in various hues, that outshone the countless stones he had scattered along the beach. While thus at work a cyclone from the setting sun swept across the great lake! Waw-saw-mo-win (lightning)[12] flashed across waw-kwi (the Heavens)![13] An-a-mi-ka (thunder)[14] in concert with ti-gow-og (the roaring waves)[15] rolled their awful burden on the land! The Earth shook! Hail and rain beat against Him! But in His majesty, He stood smiling in the teeth of the storm!

At length the dark clouds rolled away, and the setting sun lit up the passing gloom! He then picked up the giant bow that he had made, bent it across mi-ka-tik (his knee),[16] then with his breath he blew a blast that swept it eastward, between the sunshine and the clouds. As there it stood resting either end upon the trees, painting them all aglow, which in contrast with their robes of green added still more glory to the scene.

As He gazed upon its beauty and grandeur arching the departing storm, He shouted in triumph above the roaring waves in thunder tones, saying, "Kaw-ka-naw in-in-i nash-ke nin wab sa aw-ni-quod (All men behold my bow in the cloud).[17] See, it has no mit-ig bim-i-na-kwan ke-ma pin-da-wan (arrow, string or quiver).[18] It is the bow of peace. Tell it to your children's children, that Ki-ja-Man-i-to made it and placed it there that generations yet unborn, when they behold it, may tell their children that Ki-ja-Man-i-to placed his bow in the clouds without arrow, string or quiver, that they might know He loved peace and hated war."

The tradition above given was handed down to us by a tribe of Au-nish-naw-be-og (Indians)[19] that lived in Michigan before my people, the Pottawattamies. They were called Mash-ko-de (Prairie tribe)[20] on account of their clearing up large tracts of land and living somewhat as farmers. They were said to be very peaceable, seldom going on the war path. The Ottawas, who have always been very friendly with our people, tell us, they drove them out of this country and nearly exterminated them, about four hundred years ago.

We had much reverence for their traditions as we occupied the land of their principal odena (village) lying between Maw-kaw-te (Black River) and Lake Michigan. We named it Nik-o-nong, which was derived from two Algonquin words nik (sunset)[21] and o-ni-gis (beautiful).[22] It was a lovely, as well as an important place. Ki-tchi Mi-kan, the great trail over which for ages all the northern and western tribes went around Lake Michigan to and from the great Praries [*sic*] of the West, passed near this place. Traces of that great highway may still be seen along that grand sweep of country near the Lake between the Black and Kalamazoo rivers.

In the dense forest north, south and east of us were great numbers of deer, elk and bears, while duck, geese and swan clouded our waters that were swarming with fish. One half-hour's walk north of our village was a sacred camping ground where we celebrated Tchi-be-kan a-ke-win (our yearly six days feasts for the dead).[23]

During this feast bon-fires were built along the shore, casting a lurid light far out into the lake and painting the crested waves all aflame. Children, young men and maidens, fathers and mothers went about the camp, feasting and saluting one another and throwing food into the fire, and as it was being consumed, would sing, "Ne-baw-baw tche baw win (we are going about as spirits feeding the dead)."[24] This feast kept alive the memory of the dead as do the stones that rise above the white man's tomb.

Nik-o-nong in its day was quite a manufacturing Indian village. Large quantities of birch bark was brought there by canoe loads and, as it never decays, was buried in the earth for use or trade when called for. Out of this wonderful bark we made canoes, hats, caps, and dishes for domestic use and our maidens tied with it the knot that sealed the marriage vow. Sis-si-ba-kwat (maple sugar)[25] was also made and kept in large quantities in this place and sold to southern and western tribes for wampum or in exchange for pi-jiski-we-gin (buffalo robes).[26]

South Haven of the white man, with all its shipping docks and cottage crowned hills, does not in beauty compare with Nik-o-nong of the red man with its deep wild woods, its bark canoes and wagwamed shores.

Here we lived for many generations in the lap of ease and plenty; but after the advent of the white man, Nature frowned upon us. Our forests were cut down; the game became scarce and kept beyond the arrow's reach: ke-go (the fish)[27] hid themselves in deep water; the woodland birds no more cheered us with their songs; the wild flowers bloomed no more. And now all, all has changed except the Sun, Moon and Stars; they have not, because their God and Ki-ja-Man-i-to, our God, hung them beyond the white man's reach.

Pokagon does not wish to complain. Still in nin-o-de (his heart)[28] there lingers yet a love for Nik-o-nong, the o-de-na of his fathers. And now in old age, as with feeble step and slow he is passing through the open door of his wigwam into Waw-kwin (the world beyond) he must sing in his mother tongue his last song on Earth, "Nik-o-nong Nik-o-nong, nin-in-en-dam mi-notch-sa bi-naw ki-kaw-kaw-ka-naw ki-ke-tchi-twan-in nin-sa-gia Nik-o-nong (Nik-o-nong! Nik-o-nong! I shall yet behold thee in all thy glory, my loved Nik-o-nong)."[29]

Notes

1. *Ki-os-ag* is now spelled *gosnanêk* and translates to "our fathers." The term "ki-os-ak" (*gosêk*) that Pokagon uses means "your fathers."
2. *Bi-bong* is now spelled *pon* and translates to "years/winters." The term "pon" describes winters, as this is how we measure a year.
3. *Ki-ja-Man-i-to* is now spelled *Ktthė mnedo* and translates to "Great Spirit."
4. *Mi-shi-gan* is now spelled *Mshigmé* and translates to "a large body of water," referencing Lake Michigan.
5. *O-don* should be *wzagi* and translates to "mouth of a river."
6. *Maw-kaw-te* is now spelled *Mkedé zibé* and translates to "Black River."
7. *Ki-tchi-wik* is now spelled *Ktthė wik* and translates to "top point." High point along Black River does not refer to any type of throne, but more of a specific point.
8. *Ki-tchi-tchang* is spelled *thibé* and translates to "soul." The use of "Ki-tchi-tchang" means "your soul" in Ojibwe.
9. *Tchi-be-kan-a* is now spelled *thibékan* and translates to "spirit path," referring to the Milky Way Galaxy.
10. *Saw-kaw* is now spelled *mtegwagké* and translates to "forest." It is unclear what word Pokagon uses here as it cannot be found in Potawatomi, Odawa, or Ojibwe.
11. *Mit-ig-wab* is now spelled *mtegwap* and translates to "bow."
12. *Waw-saw-mo-win* is now spelled *wawasmowen* and translates to "lightning."
13. *Waw-kwi* is now spelled *wawkwik* and translates to "heaven."
14. *An-a-mi-ka* is now spelled *nemki* and translates to "thunder being."
15. *Ti-gow-og* is now spelled *tëgowen* and translates to "waves." "Ti-gow-og" (*tëgowêk*) means "on the wave."
16. *Mi-ka-tik* is now spelled *wkat* and translates to "his or her knee." The term "Mi-ka-tik" (*ni kadêk*) means "on my leg."
17. The language use is extremely broken here; it does not flow or make sense grammatically.
18. *Mit-ig bim-i-na-kwan ke-ma pin-da-wan* is now spelled *wip*, *sëbap*, *anaké bithkwan* and translates to "Arrow, string, or quiver." "Ke-ma" is an Ojibwe form of "or."
19. *Au-nish-naw-be-og* is now spelled *Neshnabéyêk* or *Neshnabék* and is the plural form of Neshnabé used to refer to a "Native American person." *Neshnabék* is more commonly used, but the contemporary alternative spelling, *Neshnabéyêk*, more closely reflects Pokagon's use.
20. *Mash-ko-de* is now spelled *mshkodé* and translates to "prairie." *Mshkodéniyêk* describes the prairie people.
21. *Bgeshëm* is how one refers to "sunset." The use of "nik" is a largely condensed form of an Ojibwe word meaning "West."

22. *Mnowabmenagwet* is how one refers to "it looks beautiful." The use of the word "o-ni-gis" and its meaning is unclear, and is not found in Potawatomi, Odawa, or Ojibwe. Pokagon uses it to describe a location, which is how this word is conjugated.
23. *Tchi-be-kan a-ke-win* is now spelled *Thibékankéwen* and translates to "to make a ghost path." The word used by Pokagon does not mean what is defined in-text but rather means "the act of making a ghost path."
24. The language use is extremely broken here; it does not flow or make sense grammatically.
25. *Sis-si-ba-kwat* is now spelled *zisbakwet* and translates to "maple sugar."
26. *Pi-jiski-we-gin* is now spelled *bzhêkéwéygen* and translates to "buffalo hides."
27. *Ke-go* is now spelled *gigo* and translates to "fish."
28. *Nin o-daw* for "his or her heart" should be spelled *wdé'*. Pokagon seems to have used a variation of *nin* and *wdé*, which mean "I" and "heart," respectively.
29. The language use is extremely broken here; it does not flow or make sense grammatically.

Summary for *The Red Man's Rebuke*

Blaire Morseau

The cultural significance of the white birch tree opens Simon Pokagon's *Rebuke*. He explains that out of this tree Potawatomi peoples made containers, accessories, canoes, and artwork. Superior to paper in durability, this medium for originally publishing the booklet—birch bark, peeled into fine, thin layers—was chosen for pragmatic, aesthetic, and political reasons. For, as he states, "but like the red man this tree is vanishing from our forests." After a brief poem about loss by the surge of American settlement on Native lands, Pokagon dedicates his work to William Penn, Roger Williams, and Helen Hunt Jackson. The following page features an engraving that was pressed into the wood—what Wisecup in this volume refers to as a possible form of nineteenth-century clip art. The engraving is of a landscape with dozens of teepees or conical wigwams, cleft by a meandering river. The peaceful scene is captioned "Chicago in my Grandfather's Days." At this point, the candor of Pokagon's writing becomes strong, deliberate, and austere. He and his fellow Native peoples "have no spirit to celebrate with you" at the 1893 World's Fair the four-hundred-year anniversary of Columbus's voyage in the great white city of Chicago that was usurped from his grandfathers in the name of development. Indeed, to do so, he says, would be to "celebrate our own funeral," and be like carousing at the graves of our ancestors.

FIGURE 7. Book cover of *The Red Man's Rebuke*, Center for History and Culture, Pokagon Band, Dowagiac, 2018.8.9, 1893.

Pokagon follows with a revisit to recent history to explain the destitute circumstances that so many Native peoples find themselves in at that point in time—in poverty, suffering with alcoholism, and experiencing severe depression in spirit. Through greed and an obsession with gold as well as an insincere practice of Christianity, Europeans and Americans repaid the generosity of Native peoples by destroying the land, air, and waters. The animals on which Native peoples relied vanished, and diseases swept through Native communities resulting in unfathomable numbers of lives lost. *Don't just take my word for it*, he explains, *cite your own White historians; they corroborate my claims.*

Despite the extent to which Pokagon and his people suffer, his prophetic accounts close the *Rebuke* with a sense of retribution. In a world beyond this one, "the shame-faced multitude" are those who doled out unfettered violence through oppression, slavery, and the selling of toxic drugs. By practicing the faith of the Whites (Christianity) sincerely while corrupt American politicians, Indian agents, and businessmen bastardize the commandments of the Great Spirit, the "children of the forest" will be delivered to the happy hunting grounds. In this conclusion Pokagon imagines an alternative future for Native peoples than that prescribed by Whites, where all Natives disappear, instead living in a world much like the beauty and serenity of a woodland paradise described in his other birch bark stories where "multitudes of beautiful stones of various color, shape and size, that in sunshine outshone tchi-be-kan-a (the galaxy on High)"; "along the shore the most beautiful woodland flowers that ever bloomed on Earth"; and "all the trees with birds that sang the sweetest songs that ever fell on mortal ears." All these, indeed, are sacred to us.

The Red Man's Rebuke

Chief Pokagon

By the Author

My object in publishing the "Red Men's [*sic*] Rebuke" on the bark of the white birch tree, is out of loyalty to my own people, and gratitude to the Great Spirit, who in his wisdom provided for our use for untold generations, this most remarkable tree with manifold bark used by us instead of paper, being of greater value to us as it could not be injured by sun or water.

Out of the bark of this wonderful tree were made hats, caps and dishes for domestic use, while our maidens tied with it the knot that sealed their marriage vow; wigwams were made of it, as well as large canoes that outrode the violent storms on lake and sea; it was also used for light and fuel at our war councils and spirit dances. Originally the shores of our northern lakes and streams were fringed with it and evergreen, and the white charmingly contrasted with the green mirrored from the water was indeed beautiful, but like the red man this tree is vanishing from our forests.

"Alas for us; our day is o'er
Our fire is out from shore to shore;
No more for us the wild deer bounds—
The plow is on our hunting grounds.
The pale man's ax rings through our woods,
The pale man's sail skims o'er floods;
Our pleasant springs are dry.
Our children—look by power oppressed,
Beyond the mountains of the west—
Our children go—to die."

To the memory of
William Penn, Rodger Williams,
the late lamented
Helen Hunt Jackson,
and many others now in Heaven,
Who conceived that Noble spirit of Justice
Which recognizes the Brotherhood of the
Red Man, and to all others now living
Defenders of our race,
I most gratefully dedicate this tribute of the forest.
Chief Pokagon

By Simon Pokagon
Pottawattamie Chief

"Shall not one line lament our forest race,
For you struck out from wild creation's face?
Freedom—the selfsame freedom you adore,
Bade us defend our violated shore."

In behalf of my people, the American Indians, I hereby declare to you, the pale-faced race that has usurped our lands and homes, that we have no spirit to celebrate with you the great Columbian Fair now being held in this Chicago city, the wonder of the world.

No; sooner would we hold high joy-day over the graves of our departed fathers, than to celebrate our own funeral, the discovery of America. And while you who are strangers, and you who live here, bring the offerings of the handiwork of your own lands, and your hearts in admiration rejoice over the beauty and grandeur of this young republic, and you say, "Behold the wonders wrought by our children in this foreign land," do not forget that this success has been at the sacrifice of *our* homes and a once happy race.

Where these great Columbian show-buildings stretch skyward, and where stands this "Queen City of the West," *once* stood the red man's wigwam; here met their old men, young men, and maidens; here blazed their council-fires. But now the eagle's eye can find no trace of them. Here was the center of their wide-spread hunting-grounds; stretching far eastward, and to the great salt Gulf southward, and to the lofty Rocky Mountain chain westward; and all about and beyond the Great Lakes northward roamed vast herds of buffalo that no man could number, while moose, deer, and elk were found from ocean to ocean; pigeons, ducks, and geese in near bow-shot moved in great clouds through the air, while fish swarmed our streams, lakes, and seas close to shore. All were provided by the Great Spirit for our use; we destroyed none except for food and dress; had plenty and were contented and happy.

But alas! the pale-faces came by chance to our shores, many times very needy and hungry. We nursed and fed them,—fed the ravens that were soon to pluck out our eyes, and the eyes of our children; for no sooner had the news reached the Old World that a new continent had been found, peopled with another race of men, than, locust-like, they swarmed on our coasts; and, like the carrion crows in spring, that in circles wheel and clamor long and loud, and will not cease until they find and feast upon the dead, so these strangers from the East long circuits made, and turkey-like they gobbled in our ears, "Give us gold, give us gold"; "Where find you gold? Where find you gold?"

We gave for promises and "gewgaws" all the gold we had, and showed them where to dig for more; to repay us, they robbed our homes of fathers, mothers, sons, and daughters; some were forced across the sea for slaves in Spain, while multitudes were dragged into the mines to dig for gold, and held in slavery there until all who escaped not, died under the lash of the cruel task-master. It finally passed into their history that, the red man of the West, unlike the black man of the East, will die before he'll be a slave." Our hearts were crushed by such base ingratitude; and, as the United States has now decreed, "No Chinaman shall land upon our shores," so we then felt that no such barbarians as they, should land on *ours*.

In those days that tried our fathers' souls, tradition says: "A crippled, grey-haired sire told his tribe that in the visions of the night he was lifted high above the earth, and in great wonder beheld a vast spider-web spread out over the land from the Atlantic Ocean toward the setting sun. Its net-work was made of rods of iron; along its lines in all directions rushed monstrous spiders, greater in strength, and larger far than any beast of earth, clad in brass and iron, dragging after them long rows of wigwams with families therein, out-stripping in their course the flight of birds that fled before them. Hissing from their nostrils came forth fire and smoke, striking terror to both fowl and beast. The red men hid themselves in fear, or fled away, while the white men trained these monsters for the war path, as warriors for battle."

The old man who saw the vision claimed that it meant that the Indian race would surely pass away before the pale-faced strangers. He died a martyr to his belief. Centuries have passed since that time, and we now behold in the vision as in a mirror, the present net-work of railroads, and the monstrous engines with their fire, smoke, and hissing steam, with cars attached, as they go sweeping through the land.

The cyclone of civilization rolled westward; the forests of untold centuries were swept away; streams dried up; lakes fell back from their ancient bounds; and all our fathers once loved to gaze upon was destroyed, defaced, or marred, except the sun, moon, and starry skies above, which the Great Spirit in his wisdom hung beyond their reach.

Still on the storm-cloud rolled, while before its lightning and thunder the beasts of the field and the fowls of the air withered like grass before the flame—were shot for love of power alone, and left to spoil upon the plains. Their bleaching bones now scattered far and near, in shame declare the wanton cruelty of pale-faced men. The storm unsatisfied on land swept our lakes and streams, while before its clouds of hooks, nets, and glistening spears the fish vanished from our waters like the morning dew before the rising sun. Thus, our inheritance was cut off, and we were driven and scattered as sheep before the wolves.

Nor was this all. They brought among us fatal diseases our fathers knew not of; our medicine-men tried in vain to check the deadly plague; but they themselves died, and our people fell as fall the leaves before the autumn's blast. To be just, we must acknowledge there were some good men with these strangers, who gave their lives for ours, and in great kindness taught us the revealed will of the Great Spirit through his Son Jesus, the mediator between God and man. But while we were being taught to love the Lord our God with all our heart, mind, and strength, and our neighbors as ourselves, and our children were taught to lisp, "Our Father who art in heaven, hallowed be thy name," bad men of the same race, whom we thought of the same belief, shocked our faith in the revealed will of the Father, as they came among us with bitter oaths upon their lips, something we had never heard before, and cups of "fire-water" in their hands, something we had never seen before. They pressed the sparkling glasses to our lips and said, "Drink, and you will be happy." We drank thereof, we and our children, but alas! like the serpent that charms to kill, the drink-habit coiled about the heart-strings of its victims, shocking unto death, friendship, love, honor, manhood—all that makes men good and noble; crushing out all ambition, and leaving naught but a culprit vagabond in the place of a man.

Now as we have been taught to believe that our first parents ate of the forbidden fruit, and fell, so we as fully believe that this fire-water is the hard-cider of the white man's devil, made from the fruit of that tree that brought death into the world, and all our woes. The arrow, the scalping-knife, and the tomahawk used on the war-path were *merciful* compared with it; *they* were used in our defense, but the accursed drink came like a serpent in the form of a dove. Many of our people partook of it without mistrust, as children pluck the flowers and clutch a scorpion in their grasp; only when they feel the sting, they let the flowers fall. But Nature's children had no such power; for when the viper's fangs they felt, they only hugged the reptile the more closely to their breasts, while friends before them stood pleading with prayers and tears that they would let the deadly serpent drop. But all in vain. Although they promised so to do, yet with laughing grin and steps uncertain like the fool, they still more frequently guzzled down this hellish drug. Finally, conscience ceased to give alarm, and, led by deep despair to life's last brink, and goaded by demons on every side, they cursed themselves, they cursed their friends, they cursed their beggar babes and wives, they cursed their God, and died.

You say of us that we are treacherous, vindictive, and cruel; in answer to the charge, we declare to all the world with our hands uplifted before high Heaven, that before the white man came among us, we were kind, outspoken, and forgiving. Our real character has been misunderstood because we have resented the breaking of treaties made with the United States, as we honestly understood them. The few of our children who are permitted to attend your schools, in great pride tell us that they read in your histories, how William Penn, a Quaker, and a good man, made treaties with nineteen tribes of Indians, and that neither he nor they ever broke them; and further, that during seventy years, while Pennsylvania was controlled by the Quakers, not a drop of blood was shed nor a war-whoop sounded by our people. Your own historians, and our traditions, show that for nearly two hundred years, different Eastern powers were striving for the mastery of the new world, and that our people were persuaded by the different factions to take the war-path, being generally led by white men who had been discharged from prisons for crimes committed in the Old World.

Read the following, left on record by Peter Martyr, who visited our forefathers in the day of Columbus.

> It is certain that the land among these people is as common as the sun and water, and that 'mine and thine,' the seed of all misery, have no place with them. They are content with so little, that in so large a country they have rather a superfluity than a scarceness: so that they seem to live in the golden world without toil, living in open gardens not intrenched with dykes, divided with hedges, or defended with walls. They deal truly with one another, without laws, without books, without judges.

They take him for an evil and mischievous man, who taketh pleasure in doing hurt to another, and albeit they delight not in superfluities, yet they make provision for the increase of such roots whereof they make bread, content with such simple diet whereof health is preserved, and disease avoided.

Your own histories show that Columbus on his first visit to our shores, in a message to the king and queen of Spain, paid our forefathers this beautiful tribute:

They are loving, uncovetous people: so docile in all things that I swear your majesties there is not in the world a better race or a more delightful country. They love their neighbors as themselves, and their talk is ever sweet and gentle, accompanied with smiles. And though they be naked, yet their manners are decorous and praiseworthy."

But a few years passed away, and your historians left to be perused with shame, the following facts:

On the islands of the Atlantic coast and in the populous empires of Mexico and Peru, the Spaniards, through pretense of friendship and religion, gained audience with chiefs and kings, their families and attendants. They were received with great kindness and courtesy but in return they most treacherously seized and bound in chains the unsuspecting natives; and as a ransom for their release, demanded large sums of gold which were soon given by their subjects. But instead of granting them freedom as promised, they were put to death in a most shocking manner. Their subjects were then hunted down like wild beasts, with bloodhounds, robbed and enslaved; while under pretext to convert them to Christianity, the rack, the scourge, and the fagot were used. Some were burned alive in their thickets and fastnesses for refusing to work the mines as slaves.

Tradition says these acts of base ingratitude were communicated from tribe to tribe throughout the continent, and that a universal wail as one voice went up from all the tribes of the unbroken wilderness: "We must beat back these strangers from our shores before they seize our lands and homes, or slavery and death are ours."

Reader, pause here, close your eyes, shut out from your heart all prejudice against our race, and honestly consider the above records penned by the pale-faced historians centuries ago; and tell us in the name of eternal truth, and by all that is sacred and dear to mankind, was there ever a peopl [*sic*] without the slightest reason of offense, more treacherously imprisoned and scourged than we have been? And tell us, have crime, despotism, violence, and slavery ever been dealt out in a more wicked manner to crush out life and liberty; or was ever a people more mortally offended than our forefathers were?

Almighty Spirit of humanity, let thy arms of compassion embrace and shield us from the charge of treachery, vindictiveness, and cruelty, and save us from further oppression! And may the greatest chief of the United States appoint no more broken down or disappointed politicians as agents to deal with us, but may he select good men that are tried and true, men who fear not to do the right. This is our prayer. What would remain for us if we were not allowed to pray? All else we acknowledge to be in the hands of this great republic.

It is clear that for years after the discovery of this country, we stood before the coming strangers, as a block of marble before the sculptor, ready to be shaped into a statue of grace and beauty; but in their greed for gold, the block was hacked to pieces and destroyed. Child-like we trusted in them with all our hearts; and as the young nestling while yet blind, swallows each morsel given by the parent bird, so we drank in all they said. They showed us the compass that guided them across the trackless deep, and as its needle swung to and fro only resting to the north, we looked upon it as a thing of life from the eternal world. We could not understand the lightning and thunder of their guns, believing they were weapons of the gods; nor could we fathom their wisdom in knowing and telling us the exact time in which the sun or moon should be darkened; hence we looked upon them as divine; we revered them—yes, we trusted them, as infants trust in the arms of their mothers.

But again and again was our confidence betrayed, until we were compelled to know that greed for gold was all the balance-wheel they had. The remnant of the beasts are now wild and keep beyond the arrow's reach, the fowls fly high in the air, the fish hide themselves in deep waters. We have been driven from the homes of our childhood and from the burial places of our kindred and friends, and scattered far westward into desert places, where multitudes have died from homesickness, cold, and hunger, and are suffering and dying still for want of food and blankets.

As the hunted deer close chased all day long, when night comes on, weary and tired, lies down to rest, mourning for companions of the morning herd, all scattered, dead, and gone, so we through weary years have tried to find some place to safely rest. But all in vain! Our throbbing hearts unceasing say, "The hounds are howling on our tracks." Our sad history has been told by weeping parents to their children from generation to generation; and as the fear of the fox in the duckling is hatched, so the wrongs we have suffered are transmitted to our children, and they look upon the white man with distrust as soon as they are born. Hence our worst acts of cruelty should be viewed by all the world with Christian charity, as being but the echo of bad treatment dealt out to us.

Therefore we pray our critics elsewhere to be not like the thoughtless boy who condemns the toiling bees wherever found, as vindictive and cruel, because in robbing their homes he once received the poisoned darts that nature gave for their defense. Our strongest defense against the onward marching hordes, we fully realize is as useless as the struggles of a lamb borne high in air, pierced to its heart, in the talons of an eagle.

We never shall be happy here anymore; we gaze into the faces of our little ones, for smiles of infancy to please, and into the faces of our young men and maidens, for joys of youth to cheer advancing age, but alas! instead of smiles of joy we find but looks of sadness there. Then we fully realize in the anguish of our souls that their young and tender hearts, in keenest sympathy with ours, have drank [*sic*] in the sorrows we have felt, and their sad faces reflect it back to us again. No rainbow of promise spans the dark cloud of our afflictions; no cheering hopes are painted on our midnight sky. We only stand with folded arms and watch and wait to see the future deal with us no better than the past. No cheer of sympathy is given us; but in answer to our complaints we are told the triumphal march of the Eastern race westward is by the unalterable decree of nature, termed by them "the survival of the fittest." And so we stand as upon the sea-shore, chained hand and foot, while the incoming tide of the great ocean of civilization rises slowly but surely to overwhelm us.

But a few more generations and the last child of the forest will have passed into the world beyond—into that kingdom where Tche-ban-you-booz,[1] the Great Spirit, dwelleth, who loveth justice and mercy, and hateth evil; who has declared the "fittest" in his kingdom shall be those alone that hear and aid his children when they cry, and that love him and keep his commandments. In that kingdom many of our people in faith believe he will summon the pale-faced spirits to take position on his left, and the red spirits upon his right, and that he will say, "Sons and daughters of the forest, your prayers for deliverance from the iron heel of oppression through centuries past are recorded in this book now open before me, made from the bark of the white birch, a tree under which for generations past you have mourned and wept. On its pages silently has been recorded your sad history. It has touched my heart with pity and I will have compassion."

Then turning to his left he will say, "Sons and daughters of the East, all hear and give heed unto my words. While on earth I did great and marvelous things for you—I gave my only Son, who declared unto you my will, and as you had freely received, to so freely give, and declare the gospel unto all people. A few of you have kept the faith; and through opposition and great tribulation have labored hard and honestly for the redemption of mankind regardless of race or color. To all such I now give divine power to fly on lightning wings throughout my universe. Now, therefore, listen; and when the great drum beats, let all try their powers to fly. Only those can rise who acted well their part on earth to redeem and save the fallen."

The drum will be sounded, and that innumerable multitude will appear like some vast sea of wounded birds struggling to rise. We shall behold it, and shall hear their fluttering as the rumbling of an earthquake, and to our surprise shall see but a scattering few in triumph rise, and hear their songs re-echo through the vault of heaven as they sing, "Glory to the highest who hath redeemed and saved us."

Then the Great Spirit will speak with a voice of thunder to the remaining shame-faced multitude: "Hear ye: it is through great mercy that you have been permitted to enter these happy hunting-grounds. Therefore I charge you in presence of these red men that you are guilty of having tyrannized over them in many and strange ways. I find you guilty of having made wanton wholesale butchery of their game and fish, I find you guilty of using tobacco, a poisonous weed made only to kill parasites on plants and lice on man and beast. You found it with the red man, who used it only in smoking the pipe of peace, to confirm their contracts, in place of a seal. But you multiplied its use, not only in smoking, but in chewing, snuffing, thus forming unhealthy, filthy habits, and by cigarettes, the abomination of abominations, learned little children to hunger and thirst after the father and mother of palsy and cancers.

"I find you guilty of tagging after the pay agents sent out by the great chief of the United States, among the Indians, to pay off their birth-right claims to home, and liberty, and native lands, and then sneaking about their agencies by deceit and trickery, cheating and robbing them of their money and goods, thus leaving them poor and naked. I also find you guilty of following the trail of Christian missionaries into the wilderness among the natives, and when they had set up my altars, and the great work of redemption had just begun, and some in faith believed, you then and there most wickedly set up the idol of man-tchi-man-in-to (the devil),[2] and there stuck out your sign, SAMPLE ROOMS. You then dealt out to the sons of the forest a most damnable drug, fitly termed on earth by Christian women, 'a beverage of hell,' which destroyed both body and soul, taking therefore, all their money and blankets, and scrupling not to take in pawn the Bibles given them by my servants.

"Therefore know ye, this much abused race shall enjoy the liberties of these happy hunting-grounds, while I teach them my will, which you were in duty bound to do while on earth. But instead, you blocked up the highway that led to heaven, that the car of salvation might not pass over. Had you done your duty, they as well as you would now be rejoicing in glory with my saints with whom you, fluttering, tried this day in vain to rise. But now I say unto you, Stand back! you shall not tread upon the heels of my people, nor tyrannize over them anymore. Neither shall you with gatling-gun or otherwise disturb or break up their prayer-meetings in camp any more. Neither shall you practice with weapons of lightning and thunder any more. Neither shall you use tobacco in any shape, way, or manner. Neither shall you touch, taste, handle, make, buy, or sell anything that can intoxicate any more. And know ye, ye cannot buy out the law or skulk by justice here; and if any attempt is made on your part to break these commandments, I shall forthwith grant these red men of American great power, and delegate them to cast you out of Paradise, and hurl you headlong through its outer gates into the endless abyss beneath—far beyond, where darkness meets with light, there to dwell, and thus shut you out from my presence and the presence of angels and the light of heaven forever and ever."

Notes

1. *Tche-ban-you-booz* is now spelled *Ktthė mnedo* and translates to "Great Spirit." The term Pokagon uses isn't the Great spirit, but is appearing to reference *Thibyéboz*, who is the first spirit you meet after crossing over into the spirit world.
2. *Man-tchi-man-in-to* is now spelled *Mthėmnedo* and translates to "devil."

Printing and Circulating Simon Pokagon's *The Red Man's Rebuke* and *The Red Man's Greeting*

Kelly Wisecup

n October 1893, the Potawatomi writer Simon Pokagon brought copies of his birch bark book titled *The Red Man's Greeting* to Chicago, where he sold them at the Columbian Exposition and World's Fair, held on the city's south side. The title page, pictured here, shows how Pokagon designed the booklet—in both its content and its materiality—to appeal to the fairgoers he anticipated would purchase his books. The title—*The Red Man's Greeting*—addresses potential readers and seems to welcome them to Chicago, part of the traditional homelands of the Pokagon Potawatomi, among other Native nations. In the 1833 Treaty of Chicago, Potawatomi leaders, including Pokagon's father Leopold, along with Odawa and Ojibwe leaders, had ceded the lands on which the city of Chicago sits. The "Greeting" Pokagon gave in his booklet's title acknowledged the desires of ethnographers and local dignitaries to understand Pokagon as a welcoming figure who, because of these familial connections to the Treaty of Chicago, could uniquely connect audiences to the city's Indigenous histories. During his October visit, Pokagon presented Chicago mayor Carter Harrison Sr. with a duplicate of the 1833 Treaty of Chicago and rode

FIGURE 8. *The Red Man's Greeting*, Newberry Library, Chicago, Ayer 251 .P651 P7 1893. For a high-quality digital image of the title page, and especially the illustration, see the copy of the *Greeting* at collections.carli.illinois.edu. A high-quality digital image of the *Rebuke* does not currently exist, but the title page illustration remains consistent across all printings of the booklets and across both the *Rebuke* and *Greeting*.

on a float representing scenes from Chicago's history, in a public performance of his connections to the city and its history.

But Pokagon's greeting was not simply a welcome—the desires of Chicago leaders and fair attendees notwithstanding. His title page pairs the *Greeting* with a recognition of the long history of colonialism in the Americas. In this way, Pokagon insists that his audience understand Chicago within a more extensive geography and timescale. Nodding to the fair's commemoration of Columbus's misnamed "discovery" of the Americas, the title page marks the 400th anniversary of Columbus's voyage with the dates 1492 and 1892. Next to these dates, the title page reproduces the popular "Landing of Columbus" image, based on an 1847 painting by John Vanderlyn that was hung in the U.S. Capitol rotunda and later widely reproduced. Pokagon makes his position on the fair's Columbian commemorations explicit on the *Greeting*'s first page, where he states: "In behalf of my people, the American Indians, I hereby declare to you, the pale-faced race that has usurped our land and homes, that we have no spirit to celebrate with you the great Columbian Fair now being held in this Chicago city, the wonder of the world."[1] If Pokagon's title invites readers into the book, his opening words urge those readers to adopt a critical perspective on the fair's celebrations of Columbus and its representations of Indigenous peoples.

The booklet's materiality complements this commentary: the birch bark pages invoke Potawatomi peoples' longstanding use of birch bark as a surface for inscription and a material out of which they made many other objects, from canoes to wigwams. While by 1893, white collectors and tourists sought to purchase Indigenous-made birch bark objects as souvenirs, for Potawatomi people birch bark was (and is) a material that represents relationships with nonhumans and with particular places on their homelands. Likewise, when used as a surface for inscription, birch bark participates in what Lisa Brooks calls Indigenous "spatialized writing tradition(s)" that connect people with human and nonhuman relations across place and time.[2] As Pokagon himself explained in the *Greeting*, his decision to publish on "the bark of the white birch tree, is out of loyalty to my own people, and gratitude to the Great Spirit, who in his wisdom provided for our use for untold generations, this most remarkable tree with manifold bark used by us instead of paper, being of greater value to us as it could not be injured by sun or water" (By the Author). *The Red Man's Greeting*'s birch bark pages materially demonstrate Pokagon's relations (his "loyalty" and "gratitude") to other Potawatomi people, to Potawatomi places and waterways, and to other than human beings such as the Great Spirit. Pokagon joined these practices of inscription and communication on birch bark with print technologies. In this way, he brought Indigenous environmental and artistic knowledge into relation with communication practices that U.S. audiences associated with modernity.

This essay describes the process by which Pokagon put together birch bark and printing technologies—including the type selected for the title page and interior pages, the printing press used to impress the birch bark pages with ink, and the "Landing of Columbus" image and other engravings that appear throughout the booklets. I ask how and why Pokagon sent the books to places like the Chicago World's Fair. This research requires that we critically reassess the most frequently circulated origin story about the *Greeting* and the *Rebuke*. First told by Pokagon's publisher, the Hartford lawyer Cenius H. Engle, and later reproduced by scholars, this story presents Pokagon as a tragic figure mourning his own vanishing and the booklets as objects that memorialize but do not complicate that narrative. In his publisher's notes to Pokagon's 1899 autobiographical novel, *O-gî-mäw-kwĕ Mit-i-gwä-kî* (*Queen of the Woods*), Engle wrote: "The old chief was present at the opening of the World's Fair, May 1, 1893."[3] As Engle had it, Pokagon hoped to see a "congress" of Native people and was saddened to see the absence of such a gathering in Chicago: "It almost broke the old man's heart." Engle located the origins of the *Greeting* in that alleged sadness: "It was in such a frame of mind he was inspired to write 'The Red Man's Greeting,' fitly termed by Professor Swing, of Chicago, 'The Red Man's Book of Lamentations.'"[4] Engle attributed the idea for the booklets to Pokagon's grief at the absence of Native people at the fair and, by extension, from the fair's vision of modernity and progress.

But Engle's origin story is undermined by Pokagon's own words in the *Greeting/Rebuke*, which refuse tragic narratives for Native people even while criticizing the terrible effects of railroads, dispossession, and alcohol on Native communities. And Engle's account is likewise compromised by notices regarding the booklets that appeared in Chicago and Hartford newspapers in early spring 1893, notices in which Engle himself played a significant role. Those articles indicate that plans to print the booklets were in place as early as March 1893, and they show that the *Rebuke/Greeting* were being printed on the *Hartford Day Spring* newspaper printing presses between May 12 and 23, 1893.[5] As a *Chicago Tribune* article indicates, the initial plan was for *The Red Man's Rebuke* to "occupy a prominent place in the Michigan exhibit" at the World's Columbian Exposition (a copy of the *Rebuke* was indeed included in this exhibit).[6] While the booklets were being printed in May 1893, I have not been able to find evidence substantiating Engle's claim that Pokagon attended the fair during that month. However, I have located evidence that the booklets were traveling to the East Coast and to northern Michigan in the months before both Pokagon and the *Rebuke/Greeting* were at the fair in October. As this archival evidence suggests, the story of the booklets' printing and circulation is much more complicated than the one Engle told.

In addition to departing from Engle's tragic narrative, this story involves Pokagon as an author even as it includes far more people than Engle's story recognized. These participants include Potawatomi people and those from other Native nations, as well as Michigan settlers and curators connected to the world's fair, who played different roles as harvesters of birch bark, makers of birch bark books, printers, patrons, and more. The processes of making and circulating the books stand not as tragic instances of Indigenous absence but as features of Indigenous diplomatic strategies in which Native people drew on longstanding artistic practices to address new contexts. This essay tells the story of some of the people who contributed to making and sharing the booklets, and it examines how audiences in Chicago, throughout Michigan, and the East Coast interpreted the booklets between 1893 and around 1900.[7]

To tell this more complex story, I ask how, when, and by whom the booklets were printed and circulated. Asking these questions helps us to break down the process of production into its parts, by considering the many hands that contributed to making and distributing *The Red Man's Rebuke* and *The Red Man's Greeting*. This question also foregrounds the many kinds of technical skills needed to produce the booklets, and the relationships that allowed Pokagon to access those skills, thus complementing the library catalog records and scholarly articles listing Pokagon as author and Engle as publisher of the *Rebuke/Greeting*. By focusing on processes of printing and distribution, we can ask a host of related questions: Who harvested the birch bark and trimmed it into thin, durable sheets? Who selected the individual pieces of type, locked them together, applied ink, and pressed the birch bark pages onto that type? Who selected the engravings that appear in the booklets from a type specimen book (the stock images of the nineteenth-century)? How did the booklets get to Chicago for the fair and to book reviewers and journalists in Chicago newspapers ahead of Pokagon's own October 1893 visit? And what happened to the booklets after the fair? What enduring uses did they have for Pokagon, and what uses do they still have for Potawatomi people?

My focus on the many people who helped to make and circulate the booklets might seem to diffuse Pokagon's authority as author, a category that often proved useful to Indigenous writers in the nineteenth century as they claimed authority to tell their own histories. The figure of the author has likewise played a significant role in the recovery of Indigenous literatures over the last few decades, as seen in excellent, groundbreaking editions collecting a single author's work (see editions of writing by William Apess, Samson Occom, Joseph Johnston, Jane Johnston Schoolcraft, Gertrude Bonnin, George Copway, and others). It is no surprise, then, that Native studies scholars have linked authorship with intellectual sovereignty. As Osage scholar Robert Warrior defined intellectual sovereignty in his 1995 book *Tribal Secrets*, "We see first that the struggle for sovereignty is not a struggle to be free from the influence of anything outside ourselves, but a process of asserting the power we possess as communities and individuals to make decisions that affect our lives."[8] In his study of Native book history, Phillip H. Round builds on Warrior's definition to show how Native people exercised intellectual sovereignty in print by positioning themselves as authors. Claiming authorship could involve obtaining copyright to their works, overseeing revised editions, and adding paratextual materials—all acts that allowed them to assert their authority in print.[9] This essay builds on Warrior's and Round's attention to Indigenous writers' exercise of sovereignty on the page, and I consider Pokagon as author even as I expand the focus on authorship to consider other Indigenous people whose labor shaped the booklets' making and circulation but who did not necessarily act as authors. This expanded frame provides a richer account of the ways intellectual sovereignty involves, in Warrior's words, both "communities and individuals."

Making and Printing Birch Bark Books

Let's begin by turning to Pokagon's copyright page. Here, we see represented one account of Pokagon's and Engle's relationship to the booklets. This page tells us that Pokagon held the copyright for the *Rebuke/Greeting* and that the copyright was obtained in 1893.

The copyright detail is significant, as it defines Pokagon as the owner of his work and ideas and establishes his relationship with the readers who interacted with the booklets.[10] Copyright was incredibly valuable for Native authors in the nineteenth century. As Round has shown, when Native writers, beginning with the Tuscarora writer David Cusick in 1826 and Pequot writer William Apess in 1829, obtained copyright for their works, their claims to ownership countered U.S. legal decisions defining Indigenous people as "wards" of the federal government, dependents who could not own or use their own land. Holding copyright was a form of sovereignty that Indigenous writers used to weigh in on the question of who owned "Indian history, Indian utterance, and Indian land."[11] Writing some seventy years after Cusick and Apess and in the context of the Columbian Exposition's claims to depict Indigenous histories,

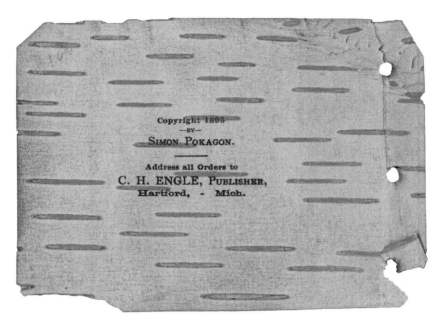

Copyright 1893
—BY—
SIMON POKAGON.

Address all Orders to
C. H. ENGLE, PUBLISHER,
Hartford, - Mich.

FIGURE 9. Copyright page in *The Red Man's Greeting*, Newberry Library, Chicago, Ayer 251 .P651 P7 1893.

Pokagon's possession of copyright is a powerful claim to sovereignty over how Indigenous peoples' pasts and futures were represented.

Alongside Pokagon's copyright, the page tells us that Cenius H. Engle, of Hartford, Michigan, acted as the publisher. This detail does not mean that Engle himself printed the booklets, but rather that he probably furnished the funding necessary for their printing (publishing and printing were separate roles in the nineteenth century). A lawyer who provided legal assistance to the Pokagon Band when it petitioned the federal government for unpaid annuities between the 1860s and 1890s, Engle was also a well-off Hartford citizen and temperance advocate. In his own written work, Engle fashioned himself as an expert on Indigenous people. He contributed a chapter on "Aboriginal History" to a 1912 history of Hartford and the surrounding region. Engle described his hunting trips and fireside visits to Potawatomi people, moments that speak to the fact that Potawatomi people would have known him from the mid-nineteenth century on. These stories also attest to Engle's desires to achieve a closeness to Indigenous people by "playing Indian," a performance of Indigeneity that, as Yankton Dakota scholar Philip J. Deloria has observed, emerges from settlers' desire to "feel a natural affinity with the continent," especially during moments of anxiety about modernity and industrialization. Settlers, Deloria explains, sought that feeling by turning to "Indians who could teach them such aboriginal closeness."[12] As we will see, Engle held a number of seemingly contradictory positions throughout his life: at times he played Indian in his search for Potawatomi people to take him hunting and in statements such as "I was something of an Indian myself and had slept in all kinds of places."[13] At other moments, such as when he notarized legal documents for the Pokagon Band's 1874 annuity petition, or when he assisted Pokagon with publishing the *Rebuke/Greeting*, Engle utilized his legal expertise and financial resources to support the Pokagon Band's sovereignty.[14] For Engle, playing Indian was not at odds with supporting the Pokagon Band's political claims, even as his recognition of the Pokagon Band's status as a political entity with treaty rights did not forestall his desire to claim Indigeneity for himself.

The copyright page allows us to begin to understand Pokagon and Engle's relationship and Pokagon's role as an author who owned his words and ideas. But it does not identify the many other people involved in birch bark bookmaking and in the circulations of those booklets to different audiences. To tell this more complete story, we must consider two birch bark books made just before the 1893 printing of the *Rebuke/Greeting* (see the essay in this volume by Oa Sjoblom and Marieka Kaye for a discussion of birch bark harvesting and processing). A year before publishing the *Rebuke/Greeting*, Engle published a similarly sized book printed on birch bark entitled *Bay View the Beautiful* (1892). Written by William A. Engle, Cenius's brother, a Hartford physician and amateur poet, *Bay View the Beautiful* is a poem praising a place where the brothers and their families vacationed and attended church meetings. Bay View was on Odawa homelands near what are now called Petoskey and Little Traverse Bay, Michigan.[15]

Like the *Rebuke/Greeting*, *Bay View* is printed on birch bark pages that are about 3 by 5 inches. As this image shows, copies of *Bay View* were tied with a ribbon woven through three holes punched on the left side of the pages, exactly as the pages of Pokagon's booklets are stitched together. In addition to the woodcut of the fan on its title page, *Bay View* features within its pages woodcut illustrations of Little Traverse Bay and other scenes (raising the possibility

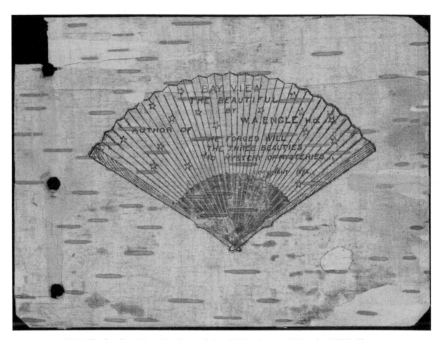

FIGURE 10. W. A. Engle, *Bay View the Beautiful*, published by C. H. Engle, 1892. Clements Library, University of Michigan, Pam 1892 En.

that the same illustrator made the woodcut map entitled "Chicago in my Grandfather's Days" for Pokagon's booklets). Printing *Bay View* likely allowed the *Day Spring* printer to experiment with printing on birch bark a year before he printed the *Rebuke/Greeting*. While I have not located explicit documentation showing that *Bay View* was printed on the *Day Spring* presses, and while C. H. Engle's location as publisher is listed in "Bay View" as Bay View, Michigan, it is highly likely that the *Day Spring* printed the Engle brothers' birch bark book. The *Day Spring* printer frequently printed items for the brothers in the early 1890s, and Bay View, Michigan, newspapers published only during summer tourist season. Working on *Bay View* would have allowed the printer to experiment with the right amount of pressure to use when pressing the birch bark pages between the type and iron press, perhaps allowing him to see how durable the thin pages were and to understand how ink reacted with the birch bark pages.

    Bay View the Beautiful seems also to have offered one textual source for Pokagon's work, for William Engle's poem opens with a short description of birch bark that Pokagon later echoed. William Engle wrote: "Out of the bark of this wonderful tree the aborigines made hats, caps and dishes for domestic use, while the maidens tied with it the knot that sealed the marriage vow. . . . Originally the shores of Little Traverse Bay were fringed with birch and evergreen; and the white charmingly contrasted with the green, mirrored from the bay, was indeed beautiful, as may now be seen along the shores of Wequtonsing. *Thanks to the pioneers of that lovely resort who spared from ax and fire a segment of nature's wreath that once decorated the beautiful shore.*"[16] Compare this with Pokagon's *Greeting/Rebuke*, where Pokagon explains his use of birch bark as a material for the booklets: "Out of the bark of this wonderful tree were made hats, caps, and dishes for domestic use, while our maidens tied with it the knot that sealed their marriage vow; wigwams were made of it, as well as large canoes that outrode the violent storms on lake and sea. . . . Originally the shores of our northern lakes and streams were fringed with it and evergreen, and the white charmingly contrasted with the green mirrored from the water was indeed beautiful, but *like the red man this tree is vanishing from our forests.*"[17] The relations between these passages are significant: they establish that Pokagon may have drawn from multiple source texts for the *Rebuke/Greeting*, in this case excerpting from and rewriting language first attributed to W. A. Engle. Or, perhaps W. A. Engle drew from materials already drafted by Pokagon. In his version, Pokagon refused to express gratitude to "pioneers of that lovely resort" but criticized those who clear-cut forests in Michigan and dispossessed Indigenous people of their lands, linking these local acts of environmental disruption and desecration to the history of colonialism across the Americas.[18]

W. A. Engle's bucolic description of the tree-lined shores of Wequotonsing referred to a place on the reserved homelands of Odawa people known as Waganakising, or "land of the crooked tree." And far from simply describing Waganakising in "Bay View," the Engle brothers were among the "pioneers" who participated in the transformation of that place into a tourist and vacation spot. Like other well-off Michigan settlers, the Engles and their families went north to Bay View during 1890s summers, for tourism and religious meetings at a Methodist tent camp. The *Day Spring* issues for 1893 include local news items that place C. H. Engle's family in Bay View all summer, suggesting that by 1893 the resort was a regular vacation spot for the families. Moreover, notices in the *Daily Resorter*, a Petoskey, Michigan, newspaper published June–September from the 1880s to 1902, indicate that in 1893, C. H. Engle was selling not just *Bay*

View the Beautiful at his "bazaar" and the local Warner Museum but also a copy of the Lord's Prayer "printed on Indian white birch bark" and "'The Bay View Columbian Greeting' . . . a booklet made of birch bark, containing a picture of the landing of Columbus, and others.'"[19]

While the printing of *Bay View* in 1892 and the other birch bark items sold by C. H. Engle might seem to suggest that the Engles initiated the idea for Pokagon's books, birch bark books are not in fact the Engles's innovation. Instead, we must trace the Engles's use of birch bark to Odawa people who were also known to Pokagon. The Odawa lands on which Bay View sits had been reserved in the Treaty of Detroit (1855), and white settlers had fraudulently appropriated those lands in the 1880s. Despite the rapid transformation of the region into a tourist destination, Odawa people continued to advocate for their rights to the reserved lands in the 1870s and 1880s, with diplomatic emissaries to Washington, DC; book publications; and local interventions.[20] Engle met two Odawa people at Waganakising who were involved in this diplomacy and longtime friends of Pokagon: Andrew J. Blackbird and his sister Margaret Boyd.[21] Pokagon and Blackbird were classmates in the 1840s at the Twinsburg Institute in Ohio, and Pokagon made frequent references to Blackbird's *History of the Ottawa and Chippewa Indians of Michigan* (1887) in *Queen of the Woods*. And relations between the Pokagon Potawatomi and the Odawa community at Waganakising were long-standing: the 1833 Treaty of Chicago contained supplementary articles allowing Potawatomi people living within Michigan who identified as Catholic to relocate to Odawa lands at L'Arbre Croche (near Waganakising). However, the United States negotiated for these lands to be ceded before Potawatomi people could move, and the Pokagon Band had to return to southern Michigan and to purchase their own homelands.[22] The cost of purchasing and paying taxes for the Michigan lands offers one explanation for the Pokagon Band's persistent advocacy throughout the 1860s and onward for the annuities promised in the 1833 treaty.

Blackbird and Boyd made and sold birch bark objects to tourists who, like the Engles, came north to Waganakising during the summer. Boyd used objects made from birch bark and adorned with quillwork as what literary scholar Daniel M. Radus calls an "instrument of Odawa advocacy."[23] In 1876, Boyd took Odawa petitions and "Indian work," including baskets, canoes, and other items settlers labeled as "curiosities," to Washington, DC, in part to pay for her train fare.[24] For President Ulysses S. Grant, Boyd brought a three-foot-long

FIGURE 11. Andrew Blackbird, *History of the Ottawa and Chippewa Indians of Michigan*, cover made of birch bark and quillwork by Margaret Boyd. E99.09 B6 1887 Archives and Special Collections, Amherst College Library.

birch bark canoe decorated with quilled designs. As Radus observes, Boyd's "birch bark containers served in the capital as they had for centuries among the Anishinaabeg: as objects that functioned discursively and socially, relaying messages and forging connections between the tribe and outsiders."[25] Boyd used birch bark for bookmaking as well: she made a cover for a copy of her brother's *History of the Ottawa and Chippewa Indians of Michigan* (1887), which the siblings gifted to Georgiana Owen, a member of the Women's National Indian Association (WNIA) who had assisted Blackbird in editing and publishing the book. The cover is made of birch bark and adorned with quillwork designs; as Radus argues, the designs "privilege . . . Anishinaabe tradition in an oft-fraught collaboration between Indigenous writer and settler-colonial editor."[26]

When we consider the Odawa birch bark bookmaking at Waganakising and the ways that Boyd and Blackbird used birch bark objects to shape diplomatic relations with U.S. heads of state, tourists, and patrons alike, *Bay View the Beautiful* emerges not as a model for the *Rebuke/Greeting* but as an object that imitated Odawa birch bark bookmaking. Boyd's and Blackbird's birch bark advocacy laid the groundwork for the *Rebuke/Greeting*, by modeling one possibility for birch bark bookmaking and by indicating how birch bark objects might be put both to what Pokagon called "domestic use" as hats, caps, and dishes, and to diplomatic use, as Radus puts it, as objects that "forg[ed] connections between the tribe and outsiders."[27]

These early episodes of birch bark bookmaking also indicate how C. H. Engle began to repackage Indigenous diplomatic materials as curiosities and souvenirs. While it reflects Indigenous birch bark practices and knowledge, *Bay View the Beautiful* elides the specific material conditions of fraudulent land acquisition that made possible the resorts where the Engle brothers and other Michigan tourists stayed and where the Engles observed Odawa birch bark work. As a souvenir for sale at Engle's bazaar, *Bay View* obfuscated the political ends to which Odawa people like Boyd and Blackbird put their birch bark objects in the service of their nation. Engle's use of birch bark to make his brother's book and small souvenir objects to sell in Bay View traded on the desires of Michigan settlers to possess objects that evoked Indigenous artistic practices without having to confront the ongoing political status of Indigenous nations, a status that was under threat for both Odawa and Pokagon Band people.[28]

1893: Printing and Circulating the *Rebuke* and *Greeting*

Despite, or perhaps because of, Engle's sales of birch bark items as souvenirs, when it came to the *Rebuke/Greeting*, Pokagon strategically used newspaper networks of printing, reprinting, and circulation in ways that diffused Engle's authority and intensified his own. We now move from the birch bark models for the *Rebuke/Greeting* to trace the booklets' printing and circulation during 1893, both before and after the Chicago World's Fair. This chapter in the booklets' story takes us to the *Hartford Day Spring* newspaper printing presses, where the *Rebuke* and *Greeting* were being printed between May 12 and 23, 1893. Pokagon may have turned to the *Day Spring* because Engle already had connections with the paper: Engle regularly paid for advertisements and notices to be printed in the paper, whether for temperance society meetings or a room he hoped to rent.

But it is also the case that by 1893 Pokagon possessed his own understanding of how periodical publication could be both useful and detrimental to Indigenous authors and Indigenous peoples more broadly. Throughout the Pokagon Band's decades-long advocacy for their unpaid annuities, Pokagon seems to have observed the speed of newspaper communication networks, the ways that placing information in one newspaper could, due to syndication networks, result in the diffusion of that information through a broader network, with little cost to the originator or author. For example, on April 27, 1892, at a moment when the Pokagon Band had finally received notice that the federal government would accept its responsibility to pay the annuities, the Paw Paw, Michigan, newspaper the *True Northerner* reported that Pokagon was up to what the article called his "old tricks." By this, it referred to Pokagon's practice of informing newspapers that the Pokagon Band was about to receive the promised annuity payment. This claim led to local speculation about whether the Pokagon Potawatomi would spend their annuities at area businesses. The paper opines:

> I notice that Simon Pokagon, the head of the Pottawatomies, is still at his old tricks and this time the editor of the Bangor *Advance* has been informed that the Indians are soon to get their money. Two years ago they were to get it, so he informed the editor of the Benton Harbor *Palladium*, and he was 'going to have the Indians paid off at the Harbor,' and the *Palladium* editor made great speculation as to how much money they would probably leave with Benton Harbor merchants. Their claim has been allowed by the Court of Claims, but how soon congress will make an appropriation for the payment is a question of time.[29]

While this quotation says much about settlers' view of the Pokagon Potawatomi annuity case as one that involved local economies and Potawatomi people as consumers—skirting if not avoiding altogether the issue of treaty rights and federal responsibilities—it also indicates that Pokagon seems to have possessed an understanding of newspapers as engines of publication and circulation. That is, Pokagon recognized how placing a news item in one paper could lead to its circulation in other newspapers, both in the region and across the United States. Indeed, news about the Potawatomi annuities was printed in Michigan newspapers and then reprinted in papers throughout other Midwestern states. This same syndication network spread information about Pokagon's booklets in the summer of 1893, and the 1892 commentary about

Pokagon raises the possibility that the annuity case provided a context in which Pokagon observed that newspapers were efficient engines of recirculation.[30]

In his use and assessment of newspapers, Pokagon participated in a nineteenth-century literary history of Native writers who turned to newspaper offices as sites for printing their literary works and who criticized the effects of inaccurate or biased news on Native communities. To take just a few examples, in the late 1820s, the Cherokee Nation purchased its own printing press in order to print the *Cherokee Phoenix* newspaper in both the English language and the Cherokee syllabary. In addition to the *Phoenix*'s advocacy for Cherokee sovereignty and homelands, the Paiute writer Sarah Winnemucca published many articles in Nevada newspapers in the 1870s and 1880s as part of her legal advocacy for her Paiute community. She seems also to have carefully used newspapers to circulate stories about her lectures and diplomatic travels. At the same time that they used newspapers as an engine of publication, Native people observed the speed and effects of periodical networks and their often-detrimental consequences for Native communities. These critiques include the Sauk leader Black Hawk's comment in his 1833 autobiography about the U.S.'s "village criers (editors)" who had falsely accused Black Hawk of killing settler women and children and then recirculated this "news" in several papers. Criticism of periodicals came as well from Indigenous intellectuals like Ely S. Parker and Carlos Montezuma, who each kept scrapbooks of newspaper clippings containing biased, stereotypical representations of Indigenous people in order to analyze those representations' material effects on Indigenous peoples.[31]

Finally, Pokagon probably also had a practical reason for turning to the *Day Spring*: the newspaper regularly advertised its services in job printing, single jobs paid for by customers like Pokagon and Engle. The newspaper would have been the closest, and probably most economical, printing press to Pokagon's home just outside Hartford. As early as 1881, the *Day Spring* ran advertisements for job printing, proclaiming that the paper offered the best job printing in the area (it was probably also one of very few local presses offering job printing). An advertisement on April 28, 1893, notes that the newspaper's foreman, Eli Irey, "has finished several contracts of job work which will compare favorably, for taste and neatness, with the best of city work."[32] And the *Day Spring* informed readers on June 9, 1893, that the newspaper "has received many compliments in regard to the graduating programs, printed in two colors, which is work seldom undertaken in country printing offices."[33] Job printing work offered a way for the *Day Spring* to remain financially solvent during the paper's many decades of new owners and fluctuating subscriptions.

In January 1893, the *Hartford Day Spring* ran an ad calling itself the "leading republican family newspaper of the United States" and reminding readers that it offered access to state and national newspapers.[34] This proclamation was more than a little inflated: the *Day Spring* was a small weekly paper of five columns across eight pages, published on Fridays.[35] The paper was frequently bought and sold in the 1880s and 1890s, even seeing a shift in ownership midway through 1893. But the *Day Spring*'s confident assertion as to its importance spoke to the paper's participation in a national proliferation of newspapers at the end of the nineteenth century, made possible by lower paper costs, increasing revenues from advertising, and efficient printing technologies that helped sustain smaller papers serving local communities.[36] This advertisement also demonstrated the newspaper's role in connecting the small town of Hartford to larger news networks through syndication (reprinting national news stories received from larger newspapers) and bundled subscriptions that offered, for example, both the *Day Spring* and a Detroit paper for a reduced rate. Even so, the *Day Spring* did not possess the newer, efficient cylinder printing presses that were employed by metropolitan daily newspapers until the early twentieth century (about fifty years after large daily newspapers began to use them). In 1893, much of the printing work for the booklets would have still been done by hand. Fritz Swanson suggests that the text for the booklets was set by hand, and that the booklets were printed on a small Gordon-style jobbing press (probably a Pearl #3, based on available printing technology and my analysis of the *Day Spring*, which describes the paper's acquisition of a drum cylinder press in the last years of the 1890s).[37] Swanson draws on his own expertise as a letterpress printer to suggest that the hand press would have been ideal for allowing the *Day Spring* printer to control the weight of the impression placed on the thin, tough birch bark pages.

After the *Rebuke* and *Greeting* were printed on the *Day Spring*'s jobbing press in May 1893, they began to travel—to Chicago by the summer of that year, but first to New York, as exhibits for the New York Press Club Fair held in June 1893. News of the booklets' travels appears in newspapers, and these notices indicate how Pokagon's relationships with Engle and Chicago Exposition curators facilitated the booklets' movements. At the same time, these reports provide glimpses of the other Potawatomi people who traveled with the booklets to both New York and Chicago; this is not a story solely of Pokagon and Engle circulating the booklets. Finally, these notices provide insight into the ways that readers received the booklets, including interpretations that sometimes followed Pokagon's critique of colonialism and sometimes read against it.

Hartford Day Spring articles from May 1893 indicate that the booklets were being printed with the plan to send them to the New York Press Club Fair, where they were envisioned as items for exhibits and as curiosities for sale. The first *Day Spring* article to mention the booklets, on May 12, 1893, reads:

> C. H. Engle has received a large order for his birch bark booklet, "The Red Man's Columbian Greeting," which is being printed at the Day Spring office, from the New York Press Club Fair, which has a large Indian exhibit, where it will be placed on sale. After May the exhibit and the Indians will be taken to Jackson Park for the World's Fair.[38]

And a May 26, 1893, article indicates that Engle and Emma Sickels, then a collector for both the Chicago and New York fairs' ethnographic departments, were corresponding about the Press Club Fair:

> C. H. Engle has received a personal letter from Emma C. Sickels, the manager of the New York Press Club Fair which is now in progress in that city, acknowledging the receipt of his birch bark booklets, which have been printed for him by the Day Spring, in which she calls them "beauties," and which will be placed on sale at the Indian exhibit of the Fair and about June 1st the exhibit will be transferred to the World's Fair at Chicago.[39]

A collector employed by Frederic Ward Putnam to obtain "Indian curiosities for the Indian Exhibit" at the Columbian Exposition, Sickels had also been a schoolteacher at Pine Ridge.[40] By spring of 1893, she had publicly broken with Putnam on his approach to representing Indigenous people and was criticizing Putnam's plan for exhibits that represented Indigenous people in a static, precolonial past. Sickels, along with members of many tribal nations, argued that Indigenous people should control their own representation at the Chicago fair by contributing their own exhibits, and Sickels tried to influence the construction of the living exhibits of Native peoples.[41] Pokagon's booklets were some of the objects Sickels sought for exhibits. And Sickels seems to have arranged for Pokagon to appear in Chicago in October 1893 and to participate in some Chicago Day events.[42]

A few months before Pokagon appeared at the Chicago fair, in spring 1893, the New York Press Club Fair was held at Grand Central Palace, then a new exhibition hall. It featured an exhibition of printing and lithography machines, a model of an Irish castle, flowers, and an "Old Curiosity Shop."[43] Sickels seems to have been instrumental in arranging for seventeen Aymara people from La Paz, Bolivia, to attend, but in a series of events that foreshadowed the mistreatment of Indigenous people at the Chicago fair, an Aymara man died while traveling from Philadelphia to New York, and the group was unable to find funding to travel to Chicago for the Columbian Exposition. The man who passed away, known in the press as "Giant Santos," was buried in New York, in a public funeral that sixty Potawatomi people reportedly attended.[44] A similarly large group of Potawatomi people were reported as visiting the fair in Chicago in July 1893, raising the possibility that the New York travels and exhibition were part of an extensive engagement with several 1893 fairs by Potawatomi people (probably from multiple communities, across the U.S. states of Michigan, Indiana, Wisconsin, and Kansas).[45] David R. M. Beck indicates that a group of sixty-two people ("Potawatomi, Sioux, Ho-Chunk") were employed as entertainers at the T. R. Roddy village in Chicago, and it is possible that many of the Potawatomi people at the New York fair were also in this group.[46] Moreover, the sizable numbers of Potawatomi people who attended both the New York Press Club Fair and the Chicago Exposition indicate that while the booklets traveled as exhibits bearing Pokagon's name as author, they were accompanied by dozens of other Potawatomi people, perhaps including some people who had harvested and cut birch bark for the booklets' pages. Much of the newspaper coverage of the fairs presents Pokagon as an exceptional figure, representing settlers' desires to position him as a link between past and present and to suggest that his education and literary output were unique for a Native man (certainly not the case). But the Press Club reports and some of the coverage of the Chicago fair indicate a wider Potawatomi presence. While their responses to and rebukes of the fairs' representation of Indigenous people were not recorded by reporters or other observers, these Potawatomi people undoubtedly took stock of the exhibitions of Indigenous lives and histories they observed in New York and Chicago. Perhaps the fairs were opportunities to reconnect with friends and relatives, or to make new connections with other Potawatomi communities. Perhaps members of these communities observed the *Rebuke* or *Greeting* on display. It may also be the case that, because Pokagon's rebuke was directed at the fairs' settler audiences, the birch bark books faded into the background for Potawatomi people as objects that were more familiar than exceptional.

After copies of the booklets traveled to New York for the Press Club Fair, news reports added to existing descriptions of the booklets as ethnographic exhibits by describing them as unique souvenirs of people and practices supposedly located in the past. References to the booklets traveled quickly through newspapers in the Midwest and across the East Coast. Such widespread circulation emerged from syndication networks that, as we have seen, Pokagon knew how to set into motion. It also seems that Engle was in touch with editors in the east, as demonstrated by reprinted articles in the *Day Spring*. In early June, the *Day Spring* carried a story about the booklets from the *New York Herald*:

We have referred before to a handsome little birch bark booklet published by C. H. Engle, which is being printed at the *Day Spring* office. It has been put on sale at a fair in New York and is thus commented on by a New York Journal.

"Among the interesting things at the Fair is an Indian book. It is a beautifully printed volume, not of paper, but of birch bark—a dainty little souvenir—entitled 'Red Man's Greeting.'

The little birch bark booklet, 'The Red Man's Greeting,' is a dainty bit of nature, breathing in every line, as well as in the texture of the leaves, reminders of the forest.

To those ignorant of the Pottawatomie Indian's poetry of thought it is a revelation. It will do much toward revealing the intellectual ability of a race who have had so little opportunity to show to the whites their love for the true and beautiful.

The illustrations bear out the thought of the chief in his review of the history of the people during the Columbian years. Chief Pokagon, the author, is the grandson of the Pottawatomie chief who ruled where Chicago now stands. His book is dedicated to William Penn, Roger Williams, Helen Hunt Jackson and Miss Emma C. Sickels, whom the Indians look upon as their friends. The booklet is for sale at the Mohawk Booth for only 75 cents a copy."

The *Day Spring* concluded by noting that the copies of the booklets were also available for sale in Hartford:

As the Pottawatomies, including Chief Pokagon, reside near Hartford and the book thus possesses a local interest, aside from its value as a curiosity, it has been placed on sale at 50c at Dr. Engle's drug store.[47]

These early reports indicate that, even before they arrived in Chicago, the booklets were already accruing several interpretations defined in part by location and audience. In Hartford, the booklets were considered objects of "local interest" that would be read by residents who knew Pokagon and other Potawatomi people personally. In New York, the *Greeting* was both an "Indian book" and "a dainty little souvenir" that carried "reminders of the forest" and attested to "the intellectual ability of a race." The booklets seem to have represented to urban readers a portal to nature and to a feeling of being close to nature, a chance to "play Indian" for a moment by holding the birch bark booklet, feeling its pages, and, perhaps, contemplating Pokagon's words.[48]

Notices of the booklets across the summer of 1893 indicate that Pokagon and Engle were taking deliberate steps to circulate the *Rebuke/Greeting*. Throughout the summer of 1893, the *Day Spring* continued to print notices of the *Rebuke/Greeting* from other newspapers, with one in August indicating that news about them was circulating widely, and that they were "being highly complimented by the press throughout the country." In a clipping entitled "The Quaint Booklet," the *Day Spring* reported:

Henry Bomrik's Bureau of press cuttings, New York, says:

C. H. Engle.

DEAR SIR:—Chief Pokagon's quaint booklet, 'The Red Man's Columbian Greeting,' is attracting considerable attention. Will you allow me to send you all notices which may appear in the leading papers of the United States and Europe?[49]

Perhaps following this trail of "notices," over the summer and fall of 1893, Pokagon and Engle were circulating the booklets and generating anticipation in advance of his appearance in Chicago for the Chicago Day festivities in October. Engle spent the summer of 1893 in Bay View, where the Petoskey newspaper the *Daily Resorter* published weekly advertisements for "'The Red Man's Greeting' by Chief Pok-a-gon Pottawatomie Indian," and listed it for sale at the Bay View Bookstore.[50] This note indicates that Engle was selling the booklets, perhaps alongside *Bay View the Beautiful*, and that they were circulating as souvenirs through tourist networks in northern Michigan.

In July 1893, Chicago newspapers begin to describe copies of the *Greeting* in book reviews that mark a turn in these interpretations. Unlike earlier accounts of the *Rebuke/Greeting* as exhibits and souvenirs, the Chicago reviews begin to treat the *Greeting* as a literary text. Like readers interested in the booklets as "a dainty bit of nature," the Chicago reviews do mention the birch bark pages, but they focus more on the *Greeting*'s content than prior accounts. The *Chicago Tribune* printed a review of the *Greeting* on July 8, 1893, in which the writer described the pamphlet as "roughly printed on fifteen leaves of birch bark; soft, tough, pliable and crudely tinted in several shades."[51] The reviewer disagreed with Pokagon's critique of Chicago and settler colonialism, writing: "But when he says 'do not forget that your success has been at the sacrifice of our home and a once happy race,' what kind of 'happiness' was that of the hapless Illinois when his tribe, the Pottawatomies, killed them almost all, men, women, and children; and what became of the 'homes' of those same Pottawatomies when the fierce Iroquois served them in like manner? Now, under our arms, peace reigns among the tribes, and we join Pokagon in demanding justice for them and wishing them all good."[52] This review foreshadows some subsequent interpretations of Pokagon's books and speeches from audiences who insisted on reading the booklets through an expectation of Indigenous vanishing and an assumption of settler superiority.

But an opposing reading appeared from journalist Teresa Dean a few weeks later. Dean, who wrote the "White City Chips" column for the *Chicago Inter-Ocean*, provided an account of receiving the booklet along with an advertisement. She wrote that "The other night there came to me a little booklet made from the bark of the white birch tree. On the cover it said: 'The Red Man's Greeting. By Chief Pokagon.' In an accompanying circular were the words: 'Red Man's Rebuke' with the word 'rebuke' crossed with an ink line and 'greeting' written above. . . . I read the little book through before retiring, and somehow its touching words made me understand better than ever before the woes and the wrongs of the Indians from their standpoint."[53] Dean went on to consider the Columbian Exposition celebrations through the framework the *Greeting* provides, understanding the fair as a celebration of a "discovery that to them [Native people] had been a death knell." After summarizing the

Greeting, she notes in closing that she received a letter "saying that the author, Chief Pokagon, who is agent for the Lawrence, Kansas, Indian school, would be here July 20."[54]

It is possible that Pokagon was in Chicago in the summer of 1893, for one purchaser of the *Greeting* wrote on September 1, 1893, that he had purchased the booklet "from the Chief." Its owner, Samuel W. Boardman (president of Maryville College, in Maryville, Tennessee), wrote that he "paid the Chief $1.00 for it; a willing bargain with a fading race." Boardman saw the booklet as a "curious production on birch bark," and he quickly donated the booklet to Harvard, writing that the booklet was "worthy it seems to me, of preservation among the treasures of Harvard; in Library or Museum which should contain all the [*sic*] relates to our Indian tribes."[55] In contrast to Dean's reading of Pokagon's account of colonial depredations and their consequences in the booklets, Boardman's understanding of the *Greeting* aligns more with the notices in New York papers, which framed the *Rebuke/Greeting* as a "bit of nature" and a "dainty little souvenir." As the booklets began to circulate in the fall of 1893, they generated contrasting readings and understandings of their significance.

Pokagon did travel to Chicago in late September and early October for the Chicago Day events, in which he participated by riding on a float depicting the "massacre" at Fort Dearborn (a battle between Potawatomi and U.S. soldiers during the War of 1812).[56] Pokagon also gave a speech alongside Chicago's mayor, which Emma Sickels helped to arrange for him. Despite his active promotion of the booklets and the *Rebuke/Greeting*'s strong critique of the fair specifically and of U.S. and European colonialism generally, newspaper accounts of Chicago Day events cast him as a figure of the past and a representation of Chicago's origin, a supposedly vanishing figure making a momentary appearance in the present. But Pokagon hardly vanished after the fair. Instead, his appearances in Chicago led to an explosion of interest in the booklets and in Pokagon himself, as evidenced by reports in Chicago newspapers and those in other cities, and by the flurry of new writings by Pokagon that began to appear in Chicago newspapers and in national periodicals.

After the Fair, 1894–99: Gifts, Material Culture, and Native American Literature

Pokagon continued to circulate the booklets after the fair and throughout the rest of the decade. This might seem surprising, for the booklets were ephemera made specifically for fairs—we might expect them to have had short-term relevance or to be discarded (indeed, I've wondered whether more copies of the books circulated in the 1890s, only to be lost or thrown out by fairgoers after returning home). But Pokagon continued to use the *Rebuke/Greeting* as gifts and as literary works throughout the 1890s.

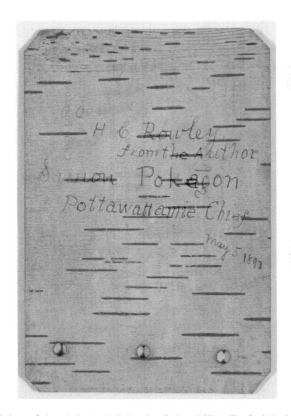

FIGURE 12. Pokagon's inscription to H. C. Rowley, 5 May 1897. In *The Red Man's Greeting*. Published with the permission of The Wolfsonian–Florida International University (Miami, FL), XC2012.09.1.1.

Pokagon inscribed a blank page of the *Greeting* to "HC Rowley from the Author/ Simon Pokagon/ Pottawattomie Chief/ May 5 1897." He sent this copy of the *Greeting* to the printing house G & C Merriam & Co.'s president, Hiram Curtis Rowley.[57] Pokagon sent Rowley as well a prospectus for his novel in progress, *Queen of the Woods*, enclosing this prospectus in an envelope printed with an illustration of himself (this illustration also appeared in promotional cards that Pokagon circulated in 1893 along with the booklets; by 1897, he seems to have been reusing the engraving on mailing materials). This missive suggests that Pokagon hoped to publish *Queen* with one of the United States' major publishers. While *Queen* was eventually published posthumously in Michigan after Pokagon's death (probably printed on the *Day Spring* presses), his use of the *Greeting* as a gift to accompany a query to a major publishing house indicates that a decade before Native authors like Charles Eastman and E. Pauline Johnson began to publish their work with large commercial publishers, Pokagon was envisioning such a publication for *Queen*. The birch bark book served in this query as another kind of "greeting," a gift to an influential publisher that Pokagon perhaps hoped would open a door to a relationship and eventual publication.

Rowley seems not to have responded to Pokagon's gift with an offer to publish *Queen*, but Pokagon continued to use the pamphlets to support the novel's publication by making copies available for sale through his correspondence with officers of the WNIA. Founded in 1879, the WNIA was an assimilationist and reformist organization that engaged in advocacy on Indian policy and supported local chapters across the United States as well as religious missions on reservations.[58] By the mid to late 1890s, when he corresponded with the Association's members, Pokagon was no stranger to such desires for assimilation, for the Pokagon Band had navigated expectations about which practices the United States considered "civilized" in arguments about treaty rights. And Pokagon had already experienced being described by news reports as an exceptional "Indian." As his October appearance at the fair shows, Pokagon was also no stranger to using those expectations and desires for assimilation to serve other purposes than those envisioned by settlers. In the case of his correspondence with Association president Amelia S. Quinton and another member, Mrs. W. C. Wood, in the late 1890s, Pokagon used their interest in what the WNIA viewed as civilization and religious instruction to raise funds for *Queen*'s publication.

An 1896 article in the *Indian's Friend* indicated that Pokagon sent a letter and napkin ring made of birch bark to the officers:

> We have recently received a napkin ring made of birch-bark, beautifully decorated [*sic*], and with the gift came the following letter: "Ki-ka-niss: Nin nin-da-i-we-ki ni-go an-an-og sa ni-ba-an-an-i e-gi-ji-gad-mi-gi-we-win Me-no-to-tom gi-ji-tchi-ga-de me-min-da-ge." (My friend: I send you to-day two napkin rings for a Christmas present. It is a good mascot, made especially for you.)—Simon Pokagon ["This ring can be duplicated, and is well worth the fifty cents for which such are sold. Orders can be sent to our assistant editor and other articles equally pretty and unique can be obtained, the avails of which will aid in the publication of the life of this distinguished Indian chief."][59]

This notice indicates that Pokagon was circulating birch bark books along with writings in Neshnabémwen (the Potawatomi language) and material culture objects, both as gifts "made especially for" women like Quinton and Wood and as objects that Pokagon offered to make available for sale to other buyers. The Association's marketing of napkin rings that could be "duplicated" suggests that the objects were part of what Elizabeth Hutchinson calls the "Indian craze," which included a desire for "Native American home decorations," many of which became part of "dense, dazzling domestic displays called 'Indian corners.'"[60] Pokagon's letter and the Association's offer to take orders for birch bark objects indicate how, at the end of the nineteenth century, the *Rebuke/ Greeting* and other birch bark items began to circulate in urban networks as collectibles and art.

The WNIA also offered copies of Pokagon's booklets for sale to its members. In April 1899, Wood was taking orders for Pokagon's *Rebuke*, offering this publication for sale alongside the history of the Odawa Nation by Pokagon's friend Andrew J. Blackbird and the Penobscot Abenaki writer Joseph Nicolar's 1893 *Life and Traditions of the Red Man*.[61] This advertisement located the *Rebuke* alongside works by other Indigenous writers, and it indicates how periodicals like the *Indian's Friend* and organizations like the WNIA helped form understandings of "Native American literature" at the end of the nineteenth century. Readers of the *Friend* could understand Pokagon's *Rebuke* alongside the tribal histories written by Nicolar and Blackbird, a move that perhaps encouraged readers to interpret the *Rebuke* similarly, as a history of specifically Potawatomi colonialism and persistence. And rather than seeing the *Rebuke* as a souvenir of the fair or as a curiosity, as Samuel W. Boardman and other readers did, issues of the *Indian's Friend* framed Pokagon's work as a work of literary interest, an art object, and a philanthropic opportunity. Finally, the fact that Pokagon sent copies of the *Rebuke* to Wood in the late 1890s is especially intriguing, as it suggests that the *Day Spring* printer may have been reprinting the booklets at that time (the presence of different title-page typefaces and layouts for copies of the *Rebuke* bear out this theory). The recirculation of the *Rebuke* rather than the *Greeting* at this moment may also have aligned with the Association's desire for works critical of Indian policy, texts that would make the case for the philanthropy the Association promoted.

Pokagon's decision to sell the *Rebuke* and other birch bark objects to raise funds for *Queen* bore fruit. In 1899, the *Indian's Friend* reported that Wood had raised $112 toward publishing Pokagon's book, through subscriptions and what Wood described as

> the sale of his exquisite handiwork, and have already a sample set of the articles, from which he will fill orders. Among the prettiest of these is a little work-box of creamy birch-bark, decorated with quill embroidery as finely worked as the best silk embroidery, and finished with dainty cords and tassels of his own making. It contains a needle-book and scissors-case to match, embroidered in quillwork and bound with fragrant sweetgrass. The little outfit is admired by all who see it. The set is $1.50, or the pieces may be ordered separately. I have also his sweet-grass mats in a variety of styles, handsomely embroidered, from 40 to 75 cents, as well as dainty napkin rings and frames. The mats are suitable for dishes and vases or perfume sachets. I have grass sachets and braids from five cents up.
>
> Would it not be a good plan for each of us to take one or more of these articles away with us on the summer vacation, and try to interest others and get orders for this worthy self-respecting Indian, who, at an advanced age sets an example of nobility and independence for his race?[62]

Illustrations of some of these birch bark, quillwork, and sweetgrass objects appeared in the periodical *The Arena*'s commentary on Pokagon's work in 1896 and in the appendix to *Queen*.[63]

FIGURE 13. *The Red Man's Rebuke*, EA 101 P761 R312 S.F., Bentley Historical Library, University of Michigan.

Such images make visible the ways that, in the late 1890s, Pokagon's booklets circulated along with other birch bark objects that were not books. Sending the pamphlets alongside napkin rings, mats, and quillworked boxes placed the *Rebuke/Greeting* within a continuum of Potawatomi literature and material culture, in which books stood in relation to—but did not replace—long-standing uses for birch bark.[64] The napkin rings, mats, and boxes likewise hint at the presence and labor of other Potawatomi people: while Wood suggests that Pokagon himself was making these items, it is likely that many other Potawatomi people were involved in their making. Subsequent articles in the *Indian's Friend* indicate that several Potawatomi households were making the birch bark items the WNIA offered for sale, and Pokagon's nieces in particular are mentioned as makers after Pokagon's death. During Pokagon's life, settlers seem to have focused on him—a focus that might indicate how successful

FIGURE 14. "Indian Splint Work," in Simon Pokagon, *O-gî-mäw-kwĕ Mit-i-gwä-kî (Queen of the Woods)*, 1899. Newberry Library, Chicago, Ayer 439 P7 1899.

Pokagon's self-presentation as author and owner of his work was. But reading between the lines and consulting later archives indicates that Pokagon was working with other Potawatomi people to make and sell birch bark items. The birch bark napkin rings and mats—as well as the birch bark books—embody the knowledge and skill of many Potawatomi people, likely women. While their names are absent from the *Indian's Friend*, as Pokagon's celebrity made him the most (and often only) visible representative of this labor to settlers, the material objects nonetheless attest to the women's presence and work. After Pokagon's death, several of these women came more into view, even as Engle began to use the pamphlets in new ways.

Afterlives: Engle's Exhibits and Intellectual Sovereignty

In the early twentieth century, Engle returned the booklets to the display case and exhibit hall. His long-standing interest in selling birch bark items as souvenirs reemerged with more frequency and visibility after Pokagon passed away in 1899. Engle served as executor of Pokagon's estate, and he seemed to have expanded that role to include not just arranging a funeral and settling legal affairs but also continuing to publish Pokagon's writings. Engle published copies of the *Rebuke* with the *Day Spring* as late as 1904, when a *News-Palladium* article reprinted from the *Day Spring* indicated that the paper's printer was completing for Engle "another edition of the last Chief Pokagon [*sic*] work, 'The Redman's Rebuke.' This edition, like its predecessors, is printed on birch bark, and will maintain the reputation which this decidedly unique literary work has achieved."[65] The *Day Spring* printer very likely also produced Pokagon's three additional birch bark booklets in 1901: *Algonquin Legends of Paw Lake* (1901), *Pottawattomie Book of Genesis: Legend of the Creation of Man* (1901), and *Algonquin Legends of South Haven* (1901).[66] Each of these booklets were printed posthumously, suggesting that it was Engle who took the stories to the *Day Spring* and saw to their printing. Also in the early twentieth century, Engle adapted *Queen of the Woods* into a play, which he titled *Indian Drama . . . "Queen of the Woods,"* and had printed on the "Day Spring Power Presses" in 1904.[67]

The texts printed in the early twentieth century initially followed some of the same routes as the early copies of the *Rebuke/Greeting*, for some of the booklets printed after Pokagon's death were sold in tourist shops in lakeshore towns.[68] And Engle made use of the networks Pokagon had established with the WNIA to circulate the booklets through the Association's local and national networks. In 1901, the Hartford Women's Club organized an "Indian Day" in Hartford, an event affiliated with the WNIA and organized in part by Engle's wife, Sara Webb Engle. Accounts in the *Indian's Friend* indicate that, after Pokagon's speeches were read by Engle and Luther Sutton (another local Hartfordian and a former editor of the *Day Spring*), guests attended a "social hour" and banquet of "Indian corn mush and milk" at which they were each "handed a souvenir of birch bark on which was printed the Lord's Prayer in Indian as well as in English."[69] The "Indian Day" events exemplify how recirculation can shade into appropriation, as Phillip Round has observed

FIGURE 15. Engle's dramatic adaptation of *Queen of the Woods*. Printed on the *Day Spring* "power presses," 1904. Harris Collection of American Poetry and Plays p1901 E585q, John Hay Library, Brown University.

in his study of how settler editors "repackaged" Native books. As Round puts it: "Indian books were often pirated and exploited to further non-Native publishers' particular agendas, intellectual sovereignty notwithstanding."[70] While such exploitation did not necessarily happen during Pokagon's life, Engle seems to have taken more liberties with the circulation, production, and packaging of the booklets after 1899.

Engle insisted that his acts of repackaging Pokagon's writings and selling birch bark material culture were for Native peoples' benefit. A February 1903 article in the *Indian's Friend* provides a glimpse into these arrangements, noting that "Mr Engle employs several families to make these goods ['Indian goods'] at their homes, and, as he says, 'is really doing a missionary work for their good and not for speculation.'"[71] A recurring advertisement in the *Indian's Friend* might suggest a reason for his insistence on his fair practices: "The Engles will send to any society literature for the program, and also send, paying express charges one way, an exhibit of Indian work valued at $100. Articles in the exhibit have price attached and can be bought if desired."[72] It is unclear who received the funds from purchased articles, and Engle's reference to his "missionary work" may be intended to refute or forestall suggestions that he was benefiting from purchases. This advertisement also indicates that Engle was creating ready-made exhibits for women's clubs and local Indian Days, drawing on his relationships with Potawatomi people in order to, as another *Indian's Friend* article put it, "secure . . . many trophies from the Pottawatomie tribe."[73]

It is also possible that Engle meant his reference to "missionary work" more literally and that he saw the sale of baskets and other objects as part of efforts to convert Pokagon Band people into the "capitalist and Christian framework" that WNIA officials privileged.[74] Such work would have aligned with the Association's desire to use the production and sale of Native art and material culture to teach Native women "the lessons of the market economy."[75] These efforts, as historian Cathleen Cahill and art historian Elizabeth Hutchinson have each shown, placed white women (and some men, like Engle) as instructors of Christian beliefs and Western domestic practices. Yet this plan did not always bear the anticipated fruit, as Native women used their artistic work to support their families. In addition, making baskets and other objects sustained Indigenous environmental and artistic knowledge, not necessarily assimilating them into Western practices. In the case of the Pokagon Band, members had adopted the signs and practices of Catholicism decades earlier as part of Leopold Pokagon's advocacy for the community to remain on lands in Michigan despite U.S. policies of removal. Engle's claims to do "missionary work" might thus have been strategically framed to appeal to readers of the *Indian's Friend* rather than reflecting Potawatomi peoples' actual relationship to Christianity.

By the early twentieth century, Engle was curating exhibits that contained Potawatomi-made items alongside Indigenous belongings from communities throughout North America. A May 1901 *Indian's Friend* story about the Hartford Indian Day suggests that Engle was engaging national markets for Indigenous belongings. The article describes an "exhibition of Indian relics and goods of Indian make" that included objects from books to tools:

Chief Pokagon's great work *Queen of the Woods* was there covered with beautifully decorated buckskin; there were articles made of birch bark, porcupine quills, beads, feathers, and grass; Indian war clubs, bows and arrows, curious pottery, stone heads for various implements, beautiful baskets of all shapes and sizes, pictures and photos of Indian characters, including a pair of moccasins that once belonged to Sitting Bull and a large bow and a quiver of arrows found on the Custer battlefield, and a multitude of other things, the whole comprising a rare collection worth a good deal of trouble to examine.[76]

The presence of objects from battlefields and possibly from massacre sites like Wounded Knee along with items such as pottery and "stone heads" suggests that Engle was participating in markets for materials obtained through military violence and ethnographic and archaeological excursions. The Potawatomi-made objects that had circulated at fairs and local tourist sites for much of the 1890s as a critique of colonialism and testimony to Potawatomi presence now appeared as part of an exhibit of "relics." Moreover, the "battlefield" items Engle included in his exhibit were regularly presented throughout the United States as evidence for Indigenous peoples' existence in a static past, or as materials that justified the United States' conquest of Indigenous nations. After Pokagon's death, Engle seems to have pursued more forcefully the narrative of Indigenous peoples' tragic disappearance that he associated with the booklets' origins at the Chicago World's Fair, taking this narrative to his exhibits and, as we have already seen, his stories of Pokagon.

Conclusion

Yet even as Engle was repackaging Pokagon's novel and the booklets, the circulation of the birch bark booklets remained tethered to and dependent on Potawatomi people and their expertise. This is apparent in the Potawatomi-language sections of the booklets printed in 1901. Engle lacked the linguistic knowledge to create these sections. This expertise is also evident in the booklets' birch bark pages and in the birch bark objects alongside which the booklets traveled and appeared in exhibits. At the 1901 Hartford "Indian Day," Engle contributed a display that featured "a collection of beautiful quill and sweetgrass embroidery on birch bark done by the Pottawatomie women, which is exquisitely wrought and really artistic when we consider that every part of it comes from the forest and is gathered and prepared by them."[77] This description is significant for its direct reference to Potawatomi women, who, as I mention earlier, must have been making many of the items sold through the WNIA throughout the 1890s and attributed solely to Pokagon. In 1903, one of Pokagon's nieces is credited with making "quill head dresses and necklaces," provided by Engle for an "Indian Day" at the Amherst Club.[78] Potawatomi peoples' practices of making and selling a host of birch bark objects mirror the work of Odawa siblings Blackbird and Boyd, as well as that of many Indigenous families in the late nineteenth century. Making baskets and quillworked items for tourist markets could justify continuing Indigenous practices deemed inappropriate under assimilation policies.[79] The presence of Potawatomi people, even in these glancing references, suggests that the Pokagon Band was employing the production of birch bark objects and other material culture objects in similar ways.

The story of the booklets' posthumous circulation is not, finally, one of Potawatomi absence or disappearance but of Potawatomi curation and circulation. Pokagon's son Charles and Pokagon's nieces continued Simon's work of making and circulating birch bark objects. An account of a "Pokagon exhibit" prepared for the "art and industrial department of the Milwaukee Biennial" and sent later to "Mrs. Potter Palmer at the Paris Exposition" contained pieces made by the "Pokagon nieces" who were also present at the "'Biennial' on American night, in native costume."[80] These nieces were probably Julia, Celia (Secsalia), and Mary Pokagon, daughters of Pokagon's son William. They were in their mid to late teens in the early 1900s, and they were spending summers in Michigan and school years at Haskell Indian School in Kansas, where they carried on Pokagon Band practices of contributing to periodicals by writing on occasion for Haskell's newspaper, the *Indian Leader*.[81] In addition, Pokagon's son Charles sent his father's works into international circuits when he sent a gift copy of *Queen of the Woods* to the Queen of Holland and a copy to First Lady Ida McKinley.[82] The books were enclosed in birch bark boxes that recall both the pages of the *Rebuke/Greeting* and the birch bark bookmaking that Margaret Boyd and Andrew J. Blackbird used for Georgiana Owen's gift.

Accounts of the birch bark box report that it was "made of birch bark and handsomely ornamented with flowers and the inscription 'Holland Queen' wrought in porcupine quills. The gift is unique and characteristic of Indian custom and handicraft." The box reportedly also included a photograph of

Charles. He also sent the book to contacts closer to home, such as his gift to "Graham H. Harris, President of the Chicago Board of Education. Through the courtesy of Mr. Harris and its publisher, CH Engle of Hartford, Mich, the Sunday Tribune is permitted to review the volume for its readers."[83] Much as Simon Pokagon drew on professional contacts and acts of gift giving to circulate news about the *Rebuke/Greeting* through newspapers, so Charles Pokagon seemed to be following his father's practice of using recirculation to make connections with powerful figures and to represent Potawatomi people as very present members of a tribal nation.

Courtesy Mrs. H. H. Hayes

BIRCH BARK BOOKLETS AND BOX

FIGURE 16. Birch bark box for gift copy of *Queen of the Woods*, and booklets, in Cecilia Bain Buechner, *The Pokagons*, Indiana Historical Society Publications vol. 10, no. 5 (Indianapolis, 1933), 331. Indiana Historical Society.

And of course, the birch bark booklets continue to circulate. In 2018, the Pokagon Band of Potawatomi brought copies of all four birch bark booklets home to the tribal archives. As the Pokagon Band's former archivist, Blaire Morseau (Topash-Caldwell) wrote, the tribal nation has been working since the booklets' return to make "these reverent objects of cultural and historical patrimony available to the community."[84] And the book you hold in your hands is yet another edition of the booklets, one in a series of copies that, as we have seen, Potawatomi people made, circulated, sent as gifts and souvenirs, sold, and exhibited. Like those older editions, this one came about through the work of many Potawatomi people, both those who wrote some of the prefatory essays included here, and those who talked with me and read this essay as part of my research process.

What object categories will this edition accrue? Will you give it as a gift? Read it as a piece of Indigenous literature and bookmaking? Did you purchase it as a souvenir, perhaps at a local institution in Michigan? Will you send it to a librarian or an influential local official? Will you read it as a book that casts a critical eye on colonialism and its ongoing manifestations? The birch bark booklets have fulfilled each of these roles in the past; this latest edition puts them into circulation in a different format. They are printed on wood-pulp paper rather than birch bark, and bound with synthetic glue rather than typeset and bound by hand. This edition circulates the content of the birch bark booklets anew, and perhaps it will also generate additional categories through which to understand the booklets and to read Pokagon Potawatomi peoples' acts of bookmaking.

Notes

1. Simon Pokagon, *The Red Man's Greeting* (Hartford, MI: C. H. Engle, 1893), 1.
2. On birch bark as part of the ways Indigenous people incorporated alphabetic writing into existing practices of inscription, see Lisa Brooks, *The Common Pot: The Recovery of Native Space in the Northeast* (Minneapolis: University of Minnesota Press, 2008), 12.
3. Cenius H. Engle, "Publisher's Notes," *O-gî-mäw-kwĕ Mit-i-gwä-kî (Queen of the Woods)* (Hartford, MI: C. H. Engle, 1899), 9.
4. Engle, "Publisher's Notes," *Queen of the Woods*, 10.
5. "Poem by an Indian Chief," *Chicago Tribune*, 4 March 1893, 9.
6. "Poem by an Indian Chief," *Chicago Tribune*, 4 March 1893, 9. Occupying a multistory building on the fairgrounds, the Michigan exhibit featured geological and natural historical specimens, mining machinery, murals depicting interactions between priests

or explorers and Native people, and a replica logging camp outside the building. During the fair, a copy of the *Rebuke* was located on the second-floor exhibit hall along with a "press exhibit" and "a collection of Michigan birds, beasts, and reptiles, woods, grains, Indian relics and minerals—everything that lives or has a being in Michigan." See Benjamin Cummings Truman, *History of the World's Fair, Being a Complete and Authentic Description of the Columbian Exposition* (Chicago, 1893), 489. See also *Rand McNally & Co.'s Handbook of the World's Columbian Exposition* (Chicago: Rand McNally & Co., 1893), 187, and reference to the *Rebuke* on 189.

7. I build here on prior scholarship about Pokagon and the booklets. See Frederick E. Hoxie, *Talking Back to Civilization: Indian Voices from the Progressive Era* (New York: Macmillan, 2001); Nancy Bentley, *Frantic Panoramas: American Literature and Mass Culture, 1870–1920* (Philadelphia: University of Pennsylvania Press, 2009), 151; Jonathan Berliner, "Written in the Birch Bark: The Linguistic-Material Worldmaking of Simon Pokagon," *PMLA* 125, no. 1 (2010): 73–91; Kiara M. Vigil, *Indigenous Intellectuals: Sovereignty, Citizenship, and the American Imagination, 1880–1930* (New York: Oxford University Press, 2015); and John N. Low, *Imprints: The Pokagon Band of Potawatomi Indians and the City of Chicago* (East Lansing: Michigan State University Press, 2016).

8. Robert Allen Warrior, *Tribal Secrets: Recovering American Indian Intellectual Traditions* (Minneapolis: University of Minnesota Press, 1995), 124.

9. Phillip H. Round, *Removable Type: Histories of the Book in Indian Country, 1663–1880* (Chapel Hill: University of North Carolina Press, 2010), 151.

10. See Round, *Removable Type*, 154–55.

11. Round, *Removable Type*, 151 and 170.

12. Philip J. Deloria, *Playing Indian* (New Haven, CT: Yale University Press, 1998), 5; and Eve Tuck and K. Wayne Yang, "Decolonization Is Not a Metaphor," *Decolonization: Indigeneity, Education & Society* 1, no. 1 (2012).

13. Cenius H. Engle, "Aboriginal History," *A History of Van Buren County Michigan by Captain O.W. Rowland*, vol. 1 (Chicago: Lewis Publishing Company, 1912), 17.

14. Engle affirmed the identities of several Potawatomi men who protested against an underpayment of $39,000 made to the tribe in 1866 and deemed (inaccurately) by the federal government as final. "Report of the Hon. S.S. Burdett Referred to in the Foregoing Memorial," S. Rep. No. 129, 51st Cong., 1st Sess. (1890), 38–41.

15. William A. Engle wrote and published several books of poetry, including a several-hundred-page tome entitled *La Pold and Euridice* in 1893; 12 May 1893, *Hartford Day Spring*, 1. On 12 May 1893, the same day it reports printing the *Rebuke*, the *Day Spring* reported that the *Day Spring* printer, Eli Irey, had "made some very fine impressions from the electrotype cuts prepared for Dr. W.A. Engle's new book of poems."

16. William A. Engle, *Bay View the Beautiful* (C. H. Engle, 1892), 1. Italics mine.

17. By the author; italics mine.

18. On Pokagon's use of excerpts from other texts, see Alex Corey, "Fair Material: Birch Bark, Politics, and the Market in Simon Pokagon's 'The Red Man's Rebuke' and 'The Red Man's Greeting,'" *Dartmouth Master of Arts in Liberal Studies Quarterly* (Spring 2010): 13–14. On Pokagon's use of excerpts from Washington Irving's history of Columbus, see Kelly Wisecup, *Assembled for Use: Indigenous Compilation and the Archives of Early Native American Literatures* (New Haven, CT: Yale University Press, 2021), chapter 5.

19. *Daily Resorter*, 26 July 1893, 1.

20. This legal advocacy continues into the present, with a recent suit brought by Little Traverse Bay Band of Odawa Indians that sought to secure affirmation of the reservation boundaries specified in the 1855 Treaty of Detroit. See the statement from tribal chairperson Regina Gasco-Bentley on the U.S. Supreme Court's refusal in February 2022 to hear this case (a decision that upheld a lower court ruling stating that the 1855 treaty did not bear on the reservation boundaries): https://ltbbodawa-nsn.gov/archive/tribal-chairpersons-statement-regarding-reservation-litigation/.

21. Engle wrote that he had "talked with [Blackbird] frequently" about Odawa stories. *History of Van Buren County*, 2. On the history of the Traverse Bay area, see Daniel Radus, "Margaret Boyd's Quillwork History," *Early American Literature* 53, no. 2 (2018): 513–37.

22. Thanks to Blaire Morseau for discussing this history in an email conversation, 4 June 2021. On the history of the treaty and the subarticle providing for the Pokagon Band to move to northern Michigan see also Low, *Imprints*, 29, and Christopher Wetzel, *Gathering the Potawatomi Nation: Revitalization and Identity* (Norman: University of Oklahoma Press, 2015), 29–30. See also Matthew L. M. Fletcher, "Avoiding Removal: The Pokagon Band of Potawatomi Indians," in *Nation to Nation: Treaties between the United States and Indian Nations*, ed. Suzan Shown Harjo (Washington, DC: Smithsonian Institution, 2014), 86–87.

23. Radus, "Margaret Boyd's," 520.

24. Radus, "Margaret Boyd's," 524. See some of the birch bark work Boyd and other Odawa women were making here: https://dcms.beloit.edu/digital/collection/logan/id/1230/rec/1.

25. Radus, "Margaret Boyd's," 525.

26. Radus, "Margaret Boyd's," 528.

27. Pokagon, *Greeting*, "To the Author"; and Radus, "Margaret Boyd's," 525.

28. For example, Michigan newspapers in the 1890s contain directions for making broom holders and other household objects out of birch bark. See, for just a few examples, "Birch-bark Broom-Holder," *St. Joseph Saturday Herald*, 23 August 1890, 3; "A Birch-Bark Stand," *St. Joseph Saturday Herald*, 17 October 1891, 3. On the ways that settlers avoid reckoning with the political status of Indigenous nations, see Kevin Bruyneel, "Race, Colonialism, and the Politics of Indian Sports Names and Mascots: The Washington Football Team Case," *NAIS Journal* 3, no. 2 (2016): 1–24.

29. *True Northerner*, 27 April 1892, 5.

30. For example, the 4 March 1893 notice of the booklets in the *Tribune* was reprinted in Illinois papers, as well as newspapers in Missouri, Alabama, and other states.

31. Black Hawk, *Life of Black Hawk, or Mà-ka-tai-me-she-kià-kiàk* (New York: Penguin, 2008), 96. Cari M. Carpenter and Carolyn Sorisio, "Introduction" to *The Newspaper Warrior: Sarah Winnemucca Hopkins's Campaign for American Indian Rights, 1864–1891*, ed. Carpenter and Sorisio (Lincoln: University of Nebraska Press, 2015), esp. 16; and Carolyn Sorisio, "'I Nailed Those Lies': Sarah Winnemucca Hopkins, Print Culture, and Collaboration," *J19: The Journal of Nineteenth-Century Americanists* 5, no. 1 (Spring 2017): 79–106. See also Carlos Montezuma, "Clippings, Scrapbook of published articles by Albert Payson Terhune, n.d.," Carlos Montezuma Papers, Box 4, Folder 219, Ayer Modern MS Montezuma, Newberry Library, Chicago; and "Ely Samuel Parker Scrapbooks, 1828–1894," Ayer Modern MS Parker, Newberry Library, Chicago. I've written about Montezuma's and Parker's scrapbooks in *Assembled for Use*, 98 and 167–70.

32. *Hartford Day Spring*, 28 April 1893, 1.

33. *Hartford Day Spring*, 9 June 1893, 1.

34. *Hartford Day Spring*, 6 January 1893, 5.

35. The *Day Spring* printed short local news items (like the notices about the booklets) on its first page, state and national news on pages 2–6, serialized stories on page 7, and "additional locals" on page 8. Advertisements for local businesses regularly occupy from two to three columns of page space, indicating the *Day Spring*'s reliance on advertising income. Midway through 1893, the paper changed hands, with Leroy S. Johnson purchasing the *Day Spring* from Charles C. Phillips in July 1893 and assuming publisher duties on August 1. In addition to the publisher, in 1893 the *Day Spring* employed a compositor, Mamie Van Ostran, and a foreman, Eli Irey. For Irey, see *Hartford Day Spring*, 28 April 1893, 1; and for van Ostran, see *Hartford Day Spring*, 23 June 1893, 1.

36. On nineteenth-century U.S. newspapers, see Carl F. Kaestle and Janice A. Radway, "A Framework for the History of Publishing and Reading in the United States, 1880–1940," in *A History of the Book in America*, vol. 4, *Print in Motion: The Expansion of Publishing and Reading in the United States, 1880–1940*, ed. Carl F. Kaestle and Janice A. Radway (Chapel Hill: University of North Carolina Press, 2009), 7–21; Carl F. Kaestle, "Seeing the Sites: Readers, Publishers, and Local Print Cultures in 1880," in Kaestle, *History of the Book in America*, 22–46; and Richard L. Kaplan, "From Partisanship to Professionalism: The Transformation of the Daily Press," in Kaestle, *History of the Book in America*, 116–39.

37. Fritz Swanson, "Cenius Henry Engle," 25 May 2021, http://fritzswanson.com/ceniushenryengle/.

38. *Hartford Day Spring*, 12 May 1893, 8.

39. *Hartford Day Spring*, 26 May 1893, 1.

40. See *Indian's Friend*, May 1892, 36: "Miss Emma Sickels is making most encouraging progress in collecting Indian curiosities for the Indian Exhibit at the World's Columbian Exposition. She has the support of a large and influential following, and the good wishes of red men and white men alike."

41. See David R. M. Beck, *Unfair Labor? American Indians and the 1893 World's Columbian Exposition in Chicago* (Lincoln: University of Nebraska Press, 2019), chap. 8 (esp. 168–76).

42. "Pokagon the Poet," *Chicago Tribune*, 4 October 1893, 1. This article includes a quotation from Emma Sickels in which she reports working with C. H. Engle to secure Pokagon's appearance at the fair. She notes that "Mr. Engle has prevailed on him to ride on our float as the chief of the Indians and to carry with him the original treaty." See also "Chicago at the Fair," *Chicago Inter-Ocean*, 9 October 1893, 13. The correspondence among Pokagon, Engle, and Sickels to which the booklets owed their travels to New York may date back at least to 1892. On 7 February 1892, the *Chicago Inter-Ocean* reported that Sickels gave a speech at the home of Mrs. [Alice] George B. Engle. This George B. Engle is likely George Junior, a cousin of Cenius H. Engle. This familial network is one possible point of connection between Engle and Sickels, and Sickels's public talks in summer 1892 about the ghost dance and the anticipated exhibits for the fair would also have made her visible to Pokagon, as plans for the Michigan state exhibit took shape. In December 1892, Chicago newspapers reported that Pokagon was in the city to speak to schoolchildren, indicating the presence of his own networks and connections in the city. The booklets' travels to New York seem to emerge out of these connections.

43. "Opening of a Big Celebration," *New York Times*, 1 May 1893, 8; "Large Attendance at Press

Club Fair," *New York Times*, 11 May 1893, 2.

44. "Giant Santos's Burial Bill," *New York Times*, 16 July 1893, 5. See also Beck, *Unfair Labor?*, 188–89; and Nancy Egan, "Exhibiting Indigenous Peoples: Bolivians and the Chicago Fair of 1893," *Studies in Latin American Popular Culture* 28 (2010): 6–24.

45. *Hartford Day Spring*, 7 July 1893, 6. Beck puts sixty-one Potawatomi people at the fair on 30 June 1893 and lists those he has been able to identify. See *Unfair Labor?*, 210. Some of these Potawatomi people may have been from communities in Wisconsin or Kansas, as well as from the Potawatomi communities in Indiana and Michigan.

46. Beck, *Unfair Labor?*, 126.

47. *Hartford Day Spring*, 9 June 1893, 1.

48. Deloria, *Playing Indian*.

49. *Hartford Day Spring*, 4 August 1893, 4.

50. See *Daily Resorter*, 8 and 26 July 1893.

51. "Today's Literature," *Chicago Tribune*, 8 July 1893, 10.

52. "Today's Literature," 10.

53. An advertisement matching this description accompanies the Newberry's copy of the *Greeting*, so it is likely that this is the copy Pokagon sent to Dean.

54. Teresa Dean, "Chief Pokagon Speaks for His Red Brethren," *Chicago Tribune*, 23 July 1893, 7.

55. Samuel W. Boardman, 1 September 1893, Houghton Library, Harvard University. Even if Pokagon was not in Chicago prior to September (which I think is likely the case), Boardman's letter indicates that the booklets were, and that they were for sale at the fair.

56. The *Day Spring* reported that Pokagon and his family left for the World's Fair on 21 September 1893, putting them in Chicago for about two weeks before Chicago Day. *Hartford Day Spring*, 22 September 1893, 1.

57. Simon Pokagon, *Red Man's Greeting*, The Wolfsonian–Florida International University. In 1897, Pokagon also sent a copy of the *Greeting* to Reuben Thwaites, then secretary of the Wisconsin Historical Society, along with a printed card featuring a photograph of himself and an account of his appearance at the Columbian Exposition. See Wisconsin Historical Society Archives, *The Red Man's Greeting*. That same year, Pokagon appeared in Chicago, at the historical society's "Fort Dearborn meeting . . . to relate the early traditions of the Windy City and the story of the fight with the soldiers Aug. 15, 1812." The historical society was "endeavoring to obtain accurate information before the last of those who connect the past with the present shall have passed away." "Traditional Chicago," *Weekly Palladium*, 12 March 1897, 3.

58. Valerie Sherer Mathes, "Mary Bonney, Amelia Quinton, and the Formative Years," in *The Women's National Indian Association: A History*, ed. Valerie Sherer Mathes (Albuquerque: University of New Mexico Press, 2015), 25–45. On the *Indian's Friend* periodical, see Lori Jacobson's chapter "'Shall We Have a Periodical?' The Indian's Friend," 46–64.

59. *Indian's Friend* 10, no. 6 (February 1898): 10–11.

60. Elizabeth Hutchinson, *The Indian Craze: Primitivism, Modernism, and Transculturation in American Art, 1890–1915* (Durham, NC: Duke University Press, 2009), 3. Hutchinson argues that the consumption of Native material culture productively complicates binaries between primitivism and modernism as artistic movements as well as between art and craft in ways that place Native people and Native art within modernity as it was defined and experienced in the early twentieth century.

61. *Indian's Friend* 11, no. 8 (April 1899): 5.

62. *Indian's Friend* 10, no. 11 (July 1898): 10.

63. B. O. Flower, "An Interesting Representative of a Vanishing Race," *The Arena* 80 (July 1896): 243.

64. On the relations between alphabetic writing and material culture objects, see Lisa Brooks, *The Common Pot*, introduction.

65. "The Redman's Rebuke," *News-Palladium*, 18 February 1904, 8. Interestingly, the copyright page lists 1893 as the date of publication in all copies of the booklets. This may suggest Engle's and Pokagon's desire to continue to associate the *Rebuke* with the Columbian Exposition, even as they printed copies a decade after the fair.

66. The Pokagon Band Archives holds a copy of *Algonquin Legends* that is enclosed in an envelope offering the booklets for sale at a souvenir dealer in South Haven, Michigan. The type and border on the envelope are identical to those used on one of the editions of the *Rebuke*, suggesting that this edition may have been printed in 1901, along with the other booklets.

67. *Indian Drama . . . "Queen of the Woods,"* Dramatized and Published by C. H. Engle, Hartford, MI: Day Spring Power Presses, 1904. Engle is reported as having completed the play by 27 January 1904 and to be seeking to stage it in St. Louis the following summer. See "To Dramatize It," *Hartford Day Spring*, 27 January 1904, 5. I have not been able to find evidence that the drama was performed in St. Louis, but the play was performed in Hartford in April 1904. See the advertisement for tickets for the play in the *Hartford Day Spring*, 30 March 1904, 4, and "'Queen of the Woods': Will Be Presented at the Academy of Music Appil [*sic*] 7," *Hartford Day Spring*, 30 March 1904, 8. See also the advertisement for an upcoming performance in *True Northerner*, 3 June 1904, 8. Engle also seems to have produced another play, *Indian Banishment*, along with his adaptation of *Queen of the Woods*. (Based on a review printed in the *Day Spring* in 1906, it seems that Engle split *Queen of the Woods* into two plays, one dealing with the forced removal of Potawatomi people from their Great Lakes homelands and one dealing with Pokagon's marriage. I have not been able to locate a printed text for *Indian Banishment*). In January 1906, the *Day Spring* reported that Engle "had a contract to put on the stage next season at the largest northern resort his two dramas, 'The Banishment' and 'Queen of the Woods' which from the present outlook will prove a great success." This article indicates that Engle continued to move between Hartford and Petoskey and to circulate Pokagon's writings (and his own productions) in both places. See "Indian Play a Success," *Hartford Day Spring*, 24 January 1906, 1. This article indicates that white actors played some of the Native characters, including Leopold Pokagon, and that at least two Black actors were part of the performance.

68. The envelope enclosing the Pokagon Band Archives' copy of *Algonquin Legends of South Haven* is printed with the booklet's title and advertising the booklet as "For Sale by S.E. Avery, Souvenir Dealer & Jeweler, Hale Block, South Haven, Michigan."

69. "Indian Relics," *Indian's Friend* (May 1901): 9.

70. Round, *Removable Type*, 174.

71. *Indian's Friend* 15, no. 6 (February 1903): 5.

72. *Indian's Friend* (July 1902): 5.

73. *Indian's Friend* 15, no. 7 (March 1903): 7. Engle sent birch bark materials and the booklets throughout the Midwest. A 1901 report from Decatur, Illinois, indicates that Engle sent birch bark books (including *The Red Man's Rebuke* and *The Pottawattomie Book of Genesis*)

along with copies of *Queen* and other birch bark items and "specimens of quill work" for an Indian Day in that town. "A Night with Red Men," *Daily Review*, 18 October 1901, 2.

74. Cathleen D. Cahill, "Making and Marketing Baskets in California," in Mathes, *Women's National Indian Association*, 126–49, quotation on 127.

75. Cahill, "Making," 129.

76. *Indian's Friend* 13, no. 9 (May 1901): 8–9.

77. *Indian's Friend* 13, no. 8 (April 1901): 5.

78. A report of Amherst Indian Day includes "quill head dresses and necklaces, made by a niece of Pokagon" and "were some of the ornaments worn by the three 'Indian maidens' who presided at the tables where these treasures, valued at more than $270, were displayed." "'Indian Day' at Amherst Club," *Indian's Friend* 15 (March 1903): 7.

79. See, for example, Alyssa Mt. Pleasant, "Salt, Sand, and Sweetgrass: Methodologies for Exploring the Seasonal Basket Trade in Southern Maine," *American Indian Quarterly* 38, no. 4 (2014): 411–26.

80. *Indian's Friend* 13, no. 8 (April 1901): 5. A *Day Spring* article reported that the Milwaukee exposition galvanized interest among women's clubs for an "Indian Day" and related exhibits, giving a glimpse into how the Engles and Pokagon granddaughters used exhibitions to generate interest in materials fashioned by Pokagon Band members: "The Pokagon exhibit given at this time, and largely furnished by women in the National Woman's Indian association, attracted much attention. Afterward it was sent to Mrs. Potter Palmer at the Paris exposition and she was so pleased with it that it was placed on exhibition. 'Since then there has been an increasing demand for material for the sporadic 'Indian Day' at women's clubs until this season it seems every woman's club on earth wants suggestions at least, and tomahawks and other things if possible"; "State Federation: Hartford People Interested in Meeting of Illinois Women's Clubs," *Hartford Day Spring*, 16 October 1901, 1. This article also indicates that Engle filled orders for such "Indian Days."

81. Thanks to Kyle Malott for help with identifying the nieces. For the Pokagon nieces' own periodical publications, see Mary Pokagon, "A Pleasant Day," *Indian Leader*, 1 March 1899, 4; and Julia Pokagon, "The Camel," *Indian Leader*, 1 February 1898, 4.

82. *Hartford Day Spring*, 14 March 1900, 5. See also "Gift Fit for a Queen," *Green Bay Gazette*, 13 April 1900, 8. Charles was also selling copies of *Queen* in Michigan tourist towns, such as Benton Harbor, and in Indiana. See "Society and Personal," *News-Palladium*, 16 November 1903, 4. And for Charles in Indiana, see "Chief Pokagon's Son Visits City," *South Bend Tribune*, 19 March 1902, 1.

83. "Chief Pokagon's Literary Work," *Hartford Day Spring*, 17 May 1899, 8.

84. Blaire Topash-Caldwell, "The Birch-Bark Booklets of Simon Pokagon," *Michigan History* (July/August 2018): 54.

Materiality and Conservation of Simon Pokagon's Birch Bark Books

Oa Sjoblom and Marieka Kaye

As book conservators, we are trained to understand and treat many different materials found in library and archival collections. This involves understanding chemical composition, historical production and use, aging properties, and the pathways to deterioration. While birch bark is more commonly found in museum collections, it is less common in libraries. The need to learn more about the history and material technology of birch bark in bookmaking arose when we each received damaged copies of Simon Pokagon's birch bark books *The Red Man's Greeting* and *The Red Man's Rebuke* at the Weissman Preservation Center, Harvard Library, and the conservation lab at the University of Michigan (U-M) Library. The damage found in the books made them unsafe to handle, and repair was required to continue allowing use. While Kaye's time is largely focused on the treatment of U-M's ancient papyrus collection, another lightly processed plant material used for transmission of the written word, neither of us were familiar with treating birch bark. To successfully treat these delicate books, we delved deep into the physicality of birch bark, and the history of how it has been handled and best preserved. We had a rare chance to work intimately with these small and beautiful books and strive to share what we gained from our hands-on work, hoping that others develop a deeper understanding and appreciation of the beauty of Pokagon's works, not just on a textual level, but on a material level as well.

Birch Bark Growth, Structure, and Habitat

Pokagon's five birch bark books are all small and short in length, ten to fourteen pages. The horizontally oriented *Rebuke* and *Greeting* are roughly three inches tall by five inches wide and only about eighth on an inch thick (approximately 75 mm tall by 126 mm wide by 3 mm thick), fitting comfortably in the palm of your hand.[1] As Dr. Kelly Wisecup describes in detail in her chapter within this book, the text is printed with oil-based printing ink in relief, referred to as letterpress. The books are oriented either vertically or horizontally, and some are made up of single pages, while others are folded pages nested together. All are bound through the left margin with green or yellow silk ribbon. While multiple copies of each publication were produced, what is most remarkable is that no two pages have the same appearance due to the natural variation in the birch bark. As noted by Dr. Blaire Morseau in her editor's introduction, users are often hesitant to handle Pokagon's birch bark books, but these diminutive books have an inherent strength. The delicacy of the individual thin layers of bark is contrasted by the strength of the bark's multilayered structure, and it makes for an incredibly flexible page.

We are most accustomed to handling books made of paper, a very different material than birch bark. Birch bark is a laminar structure made up of many thin layers; paper, on the other hand, is a network of intertwined microscopic plant fibers held together with intermolecular forces called hydrogen bonds. Although both paper and birch bark are plant-based and contain cellulose, a structural component of the primary cell wall of plants, the preparation and composition of these materials differ greatly. Historically, paper is often made with bast fibers, the inner bark of plants such as flax, hemp, jute, and mulberry, which is cleaned, cooked, processed, and macerated to form a pulp. Wood and textiles may also be processed into pulps for papermaking. In hand papermaking, the pulp is formed into sheets using moulds, which are often composed of a wooden frame with a fine mesh screen. The papermaking mould is dipped into a vat of pulp slurry and keeps the pulp contained while allowing water to drain away. Papermaking techniques vary by region and have changed significantly over the centuries with mechanization, but for a material to truly be considered paper it must be made by the formation of dispersed fibers into a sheet.[2] Other substrates, or materials that you write or print on, can be made of plant material that is not made into pulp first. Examples of such substrates include Mexican Amate bark, tapa, palm leaf, pith, and papyrus. All these materials have different properties and physical characteristics and require different considerations for conservation treatment, storage, and handling. To achieve a successful and sympathetic treatment of the Pokagon books, it was very important to understand more about birch bark and how it differs from paper, and what that means both for the interpretation of the book and its long-term preservation.

Birch is a deciduous hardwood tree (genus *Betula*, family *Betulaceae*) found in the Northern Hemisphere in areas with temperate or boreal climates, with roughly forty total species.[3] Paper birch (*Betula papyrifera* L. or *wiigwaas* in the Ojibwe language) is found in the sub-boreal forests of the northern United States and Canada.[4] There are six different varieties of paper birch in North America, and other common names include white birch and canoe birch.[5] Paper birch has oval-shaped leaves and the bark peels easier than other varieties.[6] Silver birch is a nonindigenous tree from Europe that displays triangular leaves and is most often confused with paper birch.[7] Paper birch grows as far north in Canada as Newfoundland and Labrador, across the northern United States from Alaska to New England, and as far south as the Appalachian region of North Carolina. It thrives in cold climates with short, cool summers and long, cold winters, can tolerate wide variations of precipitation, and is shade-intolerant.[8] Paper birch is also considered short-lived, with a typical lifespan of 140 years.[9]

When we say "birch bark," we are referring to the outer bark of the tree, whose laminar structure is caused by seasonal growth. Seasonal growth also leads to color differences within the laminates, with the early thinner-walled cells being light in color and rich in betulin, and the later growth cells being thicker, darker in color, and rich in tannins and suberin.[10] Betulin is the white powdery substance on the surface of birch bark, which is an antifungal triterpene. This antifungal quality, along with the natural oils in birch bark, means that it is incredibly resistant to insects and biodeterioration. It is of great interest to the pharmaceutical industry for its anti-inflammatory

  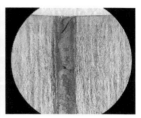

FIGURE 17. Photomacrographs (15x) in *The Red Man's Greeting* (AC85 P7565 893r), Houghton Library, Harvard University (by Sjoblom); from left to right: betulin, lenticels (inner), lenticel (outer).

and antiviral potential.[11] Suberin, an insoluble elastic polymer, also makes the bark waterproof and flexible, and makes up 85 percent of the cork cell walls.[12] The layers of the bark are held together with pectin, a naturally weak adhesive, which desiccates with age and leads to peeling or delamination.[13] The characteristic darker horizontal streaks in the bark are called lenticels, spongy areas that allow gas exchange between inner and outer tissue, and also connect layers of seasonal growth. Lenticels are commonly referred to by other names, such as hash marks, lines, and grain. Because of the permeable nature of lenticels, they lead to weakened areas in the bark, especially once removed from the tree (figure 17).

In his essay "Indian Native Skill," published in 1898 in the weekly magazine *The Chautauquan*, Pokagon described how he understood the way birch trees grow, and how they can provide material for those who work with it:

> Nature has richly provided this particular tree with two grades of bark: an inner gray bark, which runs with the grain of the wood, and an outer bark, the grain of which runs round the tree at right angles to the inside gray bark. During each year a layer of thin, tough, paper-like bark is found around the outside of the inner gray bark and under the previous year's growth. These sheets, being formed annually, cause the bark in time to become manifold; and as the tree increases in size they must grow and expand so as to correspond with the increased diameter of the tree. During springtime the various years' growth of bark can be separated and wound off in single, double, or triple sheets, so as to suit the different kinds of work desired. For some cause these sheets of bark of different years' growth vary in hues of red, white and gold.[14]

Paper birch is referred to as a "cultural keystone species" for the Neshabék for its significance in upholding cultural identity for Indigenous communities.[15] Native artists deeply understand the botanical and biological characteristics of birch bark and use them thoughtfully in their work. This understanding in Native communities can be referred to as traditional ecological knowledge (TEK) and includes direct, hands-on experience as well as knowledge passed through generations. TEK is used for understanding and planning ecological systems and land management by organizations such as the United States Department of Agriculture Forest Service's Forest Inventory and Analysis Program (FIA), through collaboration with the Great Lakes Indian Fish and Wildlife Commission (GLIFWC), in studies on birch bark.[16] TEK, as it relates to birch bark, includes the precise knowledge of when to harvest the bark, and the different properties it yields depending on the season. One such example is the use of winter-growth bark for birch bark etching, making use of the presence of a greater number of dark tannins in which to etch intricate designs. Additionally, Pokagon describes birch bark as being "used by us instead of paper, being of greater value to us, as it could not be injured by sun or water."[17] These water-resistant and impermeable qualities can be seen in the use of birch bark for canoes, baskets, architectural structures, and sacred scrolls. The betulin, suberin, and natural oils of birch bark make it a truly versatile material.

Harvesting and Sheet Preparation

Often book conservators will make mock-ups or models of objects to learn about the mechanical properties of an unfamiliar material, book structure, or treatment technique. For our treatments of Pokagon's birch bark books, we both felt this step was particularly important. As non-Natives with little knowledge of how birch bark is used by Indigenous communities in North America, we hoped to gain a better understanding of bark harvesting and how the bark is processed into thin sheets. We interviewed two Native artists who work with birch bark, and we also experimented with the material ourselves. These experiences were vital to our understanding of the books and how best to approach conservation treatment.

We were honored to speak with contemporary Native artists working with birch bark, who shared with us their expertise working with the material and answered our questions about how the thin birch bark pages of the books were likely made. The first artist we spoke to is Devan Kicknosway (Mohawk/ Potawatomi), a quillworker and YouTuber living in Montana whose work is followed by thousands on social media. His videos provide viewers the chance to learn about his artistic process, as well as other areas of knowledge. The second artist we spoke to is Kelly Church (Potawatomi/Odawa/Ojibwe, member of the Gun Lake Band of Potawatomi), a fifth-generation basketmaker and creator of birch bark bitings in Michigan, working with black ash and birch bark. Along with having her work exhibited in collections globally, she teaches widely and is an advocate for the preservation and land management of black ash. She explains on her website that creating art using black ash and birch is tied closely to "biochemistry, forest management, pest control, Indigenous language, family history, and deep, ancient connections to the landscape from which her people originate."[18] The work of these two artists speaks to the everlasting importance of birch bark to the Indigenous communities where birch grows.

To date we have found no information on who harvested or prepared the bark specifically for Pokagon's books, but we hope conversations with current artists will highlight the traditions carried over through generations of people working with birch. Wisecup's chapter in this book outlines the many Potawatomi people connected to the books' distribution, as well as those used by Pokagon's publisher C. H. Engle to sell Potawatomi art, including items made of birch bark, to groups like the Women's National Indian Association. Wisecup notes that Pokagon's son Charles and his nieces made and sold objects made of birch bark.[19] This may indicate that they, or someone in the direct family, were involved in harvesting and preparing the bark for Pokagon's books. It certainly indicates that the bark came from Potawatomi artists, or those in the Pokagon Band. Birch bark art, such as quillworking, basketry, and bitings, is prevalent in other Neshnabé cultures, and the use of the material speaks to Pokagon's heritage as Odawa, Ojibwe, and Potawatomi.

In the late nineteenth century, when the books were made, much of Michigan and the Great Lakes region were ceded. Harvesting could occur on private land, and treaty rights may have allowed the Pokagon Band access to public land as well.[20] In the early nineteenth century, the Pokagon Band was in Bertrand Township in southwest Michigan.[21] Although it was one of the only Potawatomi bands to remain in Michigan and not be forcibly removed by the United States government, the Treaty of 1833 required the Pokagon Band, led by Leopold Pokagon in 1838, to relocate north with the Odawa to a region that was called L'Arbre Croche (now considered the Harbor Springs area along Little Traverse Bay). Further treaties between the Odawa, Ojibwe, and the United States government led to the cession of this land, and Leopold and his band returned to southwestern Michigan, purchasing land near present-day Dowagiac, in Van Buren County, using annuities from land treaties. Although once more widespread, birch remains in southwestern Michigan, but is now more concentrated in the northern regions. Church, who lives and works in Michigan, noted that although birch is more prominent in northern Michigan, she believes that there would have been large stands of birch in southern Michigan as well, before the area was cleared for housing development.[22] This is seen in the use of birch for summer lodges, canoes, baskets, and scrolls in the area, showing that the material was available and widely used.[23]

In his introduction to *The Red Man's Rebuke* and *The Red Man's Greeting*, Pokagon says that the bark of his books was taken from the white birch tree.[24] From our conversations with Kicknosway and Church, white paper birch is preferred, although yellow or black birch can also be used for artistic or utilitarian purposes. Physical examination of the bark used for Pokagon's books suggests that white paper birch (*Betula papyrifera*) was indeed used by Pokagon. This bark is physically characterized by "a layered papery texture, exterior surfaces that are white or cream, matte surfaces, and dark horizontally elongated lenticels."[25] Church confirms that this is the most common type of birch used for birch bark objects.[26]

Birch bark can be harvested from live trees without affecting the health and longevity of the tree if done properly without damaging the cambium.[27] However, without proper knowledge and if done improperly, harvesting birch bark can harm the tree. Wendy Makoons Geniusz shares a wealth of information on this botanical knowledge in her book *Our Knowledge Is Not Primitive: Decolonizing Botanical Anishinaabe Teachings* (2009). Geniusz explains that the University of Michigan ethnobotanist Keewaydinoquay advised her students to only gather bark from dead trees, as most people do not know how to gather bark carefully enough from a live tree.[28] As Geniusz observed, while the tree will not die, the white bark will not grow back the same again.[29] After visiting a tree that had bark removed in past years, the new bark was rough and black where it grew back.[30] Because we lacked the proper understanding of the process, we harvested bark from dead trees to use as samples and testing for our research.

As Kicknosway confirmed, proper harvesting requires knowledge about how the bark is formed depending on the seasons and must not damage the inner cambium of the tree. Kicknosway shares a detailed video on YouTube where he demonstrates harvesting by first making a vertical cut with a knife, and then lifting the bark off with his hands.[31] If a larger piece of multilayered bark is harvested at the correct time, the harvested piece of bark can be successfully peeled into even thinner layers later. Both artists explain that properly harvested and stored birch bark can be preserved for many years and retains its desired working qualities.

The time of year the bark is harvested affects its physical characteristics. Both artists note that for making baskets, quillwork, canoes, and bitings, birch bark should be harvested in the late spring to summer months, or as Church describes, "when the strawberries are ripe." This corresponds with the time of year when sap is running through the tree, and the bark is at its thickest, making the bark easier to separate and allowing the proper time of year for regrowth.[32] Summer bark can be harvested in a sustainable way, therefore Church says that she only harvests on warm, humid days, and looks for trees that are already actively peeling, showing that the bark is "giving itself" and is ready to come off the tree.[33] She says that if harvested at the right time, the bark will make a popping sound when removed from the tree. It is particularly important to harvest in the summer to more easily get the very thin sheets of bark used for birch bark biting. Kicknosway explains that harvesting in the heat of the summer provides light-colored bark, and the heat helps with peeling the bark into thin layers. For birch bark biting, the bark is peeled into single layers. However, obtaining such a thin piece of bark is difficult to do at a larger scale, so the very fine, thin pieces remain small. This can be seen in the small size of thin birch bark bitings, compared to the thicker and larger pieces of bark used to make canoes.

Church explains that the darker winter bark, especially suitable for etching, is harvested during maple sugaring season, when temperatures go down to approximately 30 degrees Fahrenheit at night and approximately 60 degrees Fahrenheit during the day. During this season, sap is not running through the birch tree, so the bark does not separate as easily. Church does not harvest much winter bark as it can harm the tree more easily. Both artists emphasized how winter bark is less flexible and harder to peel compared to summer bark, although Church explains that heat can soften the bark and be used to aid the peeling process. Despite the challenge, it is possible to peel winter bark and use it for birch bark biting.[34]

Characteristics of the Birch Bark in Simon Pokagon's Books

Many of the pages in the Pokagon books are thin and light cream/white in color. From our conversations with artists, we may therefore identify these pages as summer bark. However, after looking at images of the books, Church also identified some pages that were darker orange and thicker, which indicates winter bark (figure 18). Since the thin, flexible summer bark is better suited for book pages, which are repeatedly flexed during use, the possible inclusion of winter bark for these books is interesting to note. The inclusion of winter bark

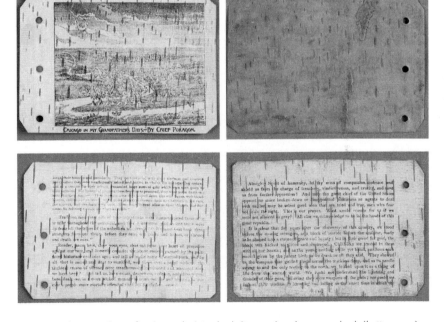

FIGURE 18. A comparison of estimated winter bark (*top row*) and summer bark (*bottom row*). Note that although the outer layer (*left*) of both barks is light in color, the inner layer (*right*) is significantly darker for the inner layer of the winter bark.

may suggest that due to the large amount of birch bark required for the printing of all of Pokagon's works, the people working on the books used whatever bark they had on hand, whether it was in storage or harvested at the time of book manufacture. Since it is known that the Pokagon Band of Potawatomi actively made objects out of birch bark for the nineteenth-century tourist trade, and birch bark can be stored for several years, there was likely a stock of birch bark available to Pokagon and Engle for making these books. However, with growing demand for the books corresponding with the 1893 World's Columbian Exposition in Chicago, sources of the thinner, lighter, and more flexible bark may have been rapidly depleted, thus requiring the use of the darker, thicker, less-flexible bark as well. We cannot make any correlation between the birch bark harvesting and the chronology of book production without careful examination of more copies of the books, so it remains an opportunity for further research.[35]

Speaking to Kicknosway and Church also gave us a better understanding of what part of the bark was used. Church shared samples of harvested birch bark, which show that the outer layers of the bark are more exfoliated and wispier, and the color is a grayish white. The innermost layer, closer to the cambium, is darker and less matte. The central layers have the most even appearance. For many birch bark artworks, only the finer and smooth central layers of the bark are used. Color can also be influenced by the age of the tree, with older trees yielding bark of a darker color, and Kicknosway explained that trees need to be at least ten to twelve years old to yield usable bark.

The delicate thinness of the pages surprised us when we first encountered these books, but after speaking with the artists we gained understanding that thin birch bark is regularly used for art, and the thin bark can hold up to strain. Church folds single layers of bark multiple times to make her intricate bitings. Kicknosway gave an example of his ceremonial hair ties, which consist of a thin layer of quilled birch bark, and how they are not harmed by the movement they go through during his powwow dances.

Lenticels are another feature influenced by the age of the tree, growing larger with age. Looking at examples of Pokagon's books, there is a wide range of lenticel sizes and density. Since lenticels are weak areas in the bark, both artists spoke of selecting bark with fewer or finer lenticels for their work. The presence of large and dense lenticels in many of these pages once again suggests that the book producers were using any bark that was available and that they could find, and that the demand for the books was such that compromises were made when selecting the bark. Natural characteristics such as knots, holes, uneven delamination, large lenticels, and darker color all affect the legibility of the text, but also contribute to the unique handmade quality of each book.

Bookbinding Structures

Before diving into the specific bookbinding structures of Pokagon's works, it is first necessary to define what a book, or what we often refer to as a codex, really entails. Jonathan Berliner (2010) gives a meaningful explanation of how closely linked birch bark and the book form have been throughout history. He writes that according to the *Oxford Latin Dictionary*, *liber*, the root word for book across Romance languages, means the inside bark of a tree.[36] Additionally, the English word codex derives from the Latin term for the trunk of a tree, and was evolved to describe many sheets of "bark bound together."[37]

Pokagon clearly explains why he chose birch bark for his books in the *The Red Man's Rebuke* and *The Red Man's Greeting*, which you will find directly transcribed in this book, but he does not discuss the bookbinding structures. Morseau writes in her article for *Michigan History*, "While not explicitly mentioned in his texts, Pokagon's use of birch paper to print his works also hints to birch-bark scrolls used by Neshabék across the Great Lakes. Those scrolls were and continue to be used to transcribe oral histories, stories, ceremonial knowledge, and other important information through pictographs."[38] Berliner also reflects on Pokagon's decision to use the book rather than scroll format, writing that "the booklet format would have been more widely recognizable to his readers as a text; with the document title and image on its cover, the work announces itself as a piece of writing and could not be mistaken for simply a birch-bark object. The intended audience is also an important difference between the Algonquian scrolls and Pokagon's booklets. *The Red Man's Rebuke* was sold at the fair to a largely white general audience, while the traditional texts were meant to be read only by a select few within the Native communities."[39]

Two types of codex structures were chosen for Pokagon's books: loose pages oversewn along one edge,[40] and folded sheets nested together and oversewn on one edge.[41] In many binding traditions, short texts are often bound as pamphlets, which consist of a group of folded pages, called folios or bifolium, nested together and sewn through the center fold in a figure-eight pattern,

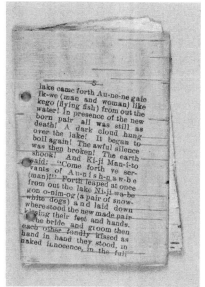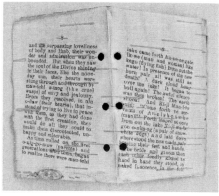

FIGURE 19. Example of a folded page (*left*) and the same page unfolded (*right*) from *Pottawattamie Book of Genesis*, University of Michigan Library, Special Collections Research Center.

known as a pamphlet stitch. The qualities of the substrate often dictate the type of sewing chosen to hold the pages together in a book. East Asian books are often oversewn through the right side (also referred to as side-sewn), but in East Asia bookbinders make use of thin and flexible long-fibered paper for the textblock pages, which open and drape easily, and readily hold up to flexing. Handmade Western paper, such as paper historically manufactured and used in Europe and the settler-colonialist population of North America, is thicker, with less drape, making it less suitable for oversewn structures. The same problems can be seen when birch bark is used for an oversewn structure. Oversewing drastically alters how the book functions; in a pamphlet, the fold in the center of the textblock allows for the book to drape open in a wider, gentler manner, but in an oversewn structure, the pages flex against the bound edge, causing extra strain during use. Oversewing the pages in this manner often results in a book that is more difficult to open and read, due to the elimination of margins in the center of the book, and can lead to splits and breaks along the bound edge, and in this case the birch bark pages weaken and break where they flex against the ribbon. The Pokagon books in a vertical format (*Pottawattamie Book of Genesis, Algonquin Legends of Paw Paw Lake, Algonquin Legends of South Haven*) are made of nested folios, and it is interesting that they are oversewn, instead of being sewn together through the center fold using the pamphlet stitch (figure 19).

We looked at other examples of books made of birch bark to see what other types of bookbinding structures were in use, and how the type of binding correlates with damage to the bark pages. The most prevalent use of birch bark for books was found in the Kashmir region of India. These books were often bound in codex form, with multiple folios nested together to make sections. The sections are then sewn through the folds connecting neighboring sections with a link stitch to form a thick and cohesive textblock. These books have damage along the folds, where the pages flex when opened, and where holes were pierced to pass the sewing thread, along with splits and delamination from aging and use.[42] In our search for other North American birch bark binding examples, we came across several created by Native artists, which involve quillworked covers, edges bound in sweetgrass, and paper or birch bark pages. One such example can be found on Wiwkwébthëgen, the Pokagon Band's digital archives site, where they shared images of a book with quilled birch bark covers and bark pages.[43] Margaret Boyd's quilled birch bark covers on a copy of *The History of the Ottawa and Chippewa Indians of Michigan*, written by her brother Andrew Blackbird and published in 1887, is a significant and very unique example of North American birch bark used in bookbinding.[44] Boyd's birch bark covers were integrated with a traditional nineteenth-century European-style leather binding and paper textblock, which is a focus of Daniel Radus's essay "Margaret Boyd's Quillwork History."[45]

We also found examples of birch bark books created by non-Native artists of the time, which are in both oversewn and pamphlet-sewn forms. One such example includes the two volumes of small poetry books by Charles Lummis, printed in 1882 and 1883, ten years prior to Pokagon's *The Red Man's Rebuke* and *The Red Man's Greeting*. Lummis's poems began as a summer project in his college years at Harvard when during his summers he worked at the Profile House in the White Mountains as the in-house printer of menus and programs and he became skilled enough to do his own projects on the side.[46] He made about a dozen different little books to sell for 25 cents each in the Profile House gift shop. Lummis's books are sewn pamphlet-style, with nested folios sewn together through the center fold with simple linen thread. Another interesting example is a small souvenir book titled *Bayview the Beautiful,* written by W. A. Engle and printed and published by his brother C. H. Engle in 1892, before Pokagon's works were created.[47] This tiny souvenir book is bound in the same style as Pokagon's horizontally oriented birch bark books with loose sheets punched through the left margin and bound together with a ribbon. Because of the C. H. Engle's known connection with the Pokagon Band at this time, it is not clear who inspired this style of binding, Engle or Pokagon community members, or if it was collaborative. Examples of Lummis's pamphlet-stitched books, as viewed in person and digitally, have less damage associated with the binding structure, but Engle's oversewn book suffers from similar damage as Pokagon's horizontally formatted books.

The grain direction, also the direction the lenticels run, influences the openability and physical condition of the bookbinding structures. In Pokagon's books, most of the breaks follow the direction of the lenticels, which is especially detrimental when the lenticels run vertically in the direction the page bends when it is turned. Paper, which also has a grain (the direction in which a majority of fibers are oriented), follows this same pattern of wear, tearing more easily with the grain. The presence of the lenticels makes birch bark particularly weak and likely to split with the grain because they are permeable areas of the bark, and thus there is not a solid material within those small lines. Since lenticels are the weakest area of the bark, piercing this area, when sewing books or creating quillwork, can lead to splits. Kicknosway emphasized the struggle working around lenticels when he spoke to us about his quillwork. The use of large punched holes to accommodate the thick ribbon for Pokagon's bindings further jeopardizes the stability and attachment of the pages (figure 20). The trouble with flexing is not always something birch bark artists need to take into consideration, as Church noted that most birch bark artwork is made to be restrained and not flex, such as the rigid sewing around the rims of baskets to prevent movement.

Printing on Birch Bark

Wisecup's chapter discusses how the books were printed at the local newspaper, the *Hartford Day Spring,* as hired job printing, and examines the typography

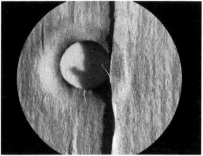

FIGURE 20. These images show punched holes and a broken area within a lenticel. The combination of vertical lenticels and the birch bark page flexing at the oversewing leads to splits in the page. Photomacrographs (15x) in *The Red Man's Greeting* (AC85 P7565 893r); Houghton Library, Harvard University (by Sjoblom).

and stylistic changes between copies to better understand the process of publishing the books. When examining the physical attributes and condition of the books, the unique qualities of printing on birch bark stood out to us as very unusual. The commonly uneven surface of the bark greatly influenced the quality of the printed text and images. As Wisecup describes, these books were letterpress printed, a commercial relief printing process. Relief printing uses a raised printing surface that picks up a viscous oil-based ink, resulting in text and images that are impressed into the surface of the page using pressure from a press.[48] The text was printed from raised metal type, and the illustrations were printed using stereotyped metal plates copied from wood engravings.

The use of pressure to transfer the inked images means that the differences in bark thickness influenced the printing quality. This can be seen in pages with uneven surfaces, layers, knots, or other imperfections. As a result, the ink is often lighter in lower surface areas, and sometimes the ink was completely unable to reach the page at all. Historically in relief printmaking processes, the paper was dampened to allow for a slight stretch around the metal to achieve a better impression. The deepness of the printed impression is referred to as the "bite," and when done properly, results in a rich, dark, legible printed text or image. Because birch bark is naturally water-resistant, it does not respond to dampening in the same way as paper, so any applied moisture would not aid the impression of the ink. We observed a large range

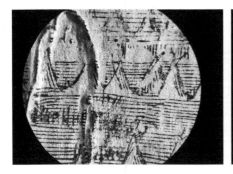

FIGURE 21. Examples of a light bite where the text sits only on the highest points due to the uneven surface (left) compared to a heavy printing bite where the text is deeply impressed in the page (right). Photomacrographs (15x) from *The Red Man's Greeting* (AC85 P7565 893r); Houghton Library, Harvard University (by Sjoblom).

of bite depth in Pokagon's booklets, with some pages printed so lightly as to be difficult to read, while others were printed more deeply. While the depth of the bite depends on the evenness and quality of the bark, it also depends on the quality of the metal type and plates and can indicate the skill level of the printer. Pressure that was too lightly applied leads to missing ink, but on the other hand, text printed with too much pressure can lead to a damaged surface (figure 21).

The uneven surface quality of birch bark is not the only detail to note in relation to the printing of Pokagon's books. In nineteenth-century hand printing, such as at the *Hartford Day Spring*, it was common for multiple book or newspaper pages to be printed at once, on one larger sheet of paper, to make a large job fast and efficient. After printing, the larger page was folded and trimmed to make separate pages. However, given the limitations in size when harvesting and peeling usable layers of thin birch bark, this process was unlikely for Pokagon's books. Instead, the pages were first cut to their desired size and printed individually, which required much more time than the usual mechanized and automated commercial printing processes of the day. It would have been possible to print the pages on slightly larger sheets of bark and then trim the pages, but due to the number of pages with text printed unevenly and at an angle in many copies of the books, this was not likely to have been the case.[49]

Treatment

The significance of birch bark to the Neshnabé people is expressed by Pokagon in his texts and was a starting point for our understanding of the history and meaning of the material more broadly so that we could execute the most culturally sensitive conservation treatment. Pokagon writes, "My object in publishing 'The Red Man's Rebuke' on the bark of the white birch tree is out of loyalty to my own people, and gratitude to the Great Spirit, who in his wisdom provided for our use for untold generations, this most remarkable tree with manifold bark used by us instead of paper, being of greater value to us, as it could not be injured by sun or water."[50] Although these books are of incredible historic and cultural significance, they are not considered sacred objects, subject to the Native American Graves Protection and Repatriation Act (NAGPRA), and there were no specific cultural guidelines for treatment and handling.[51] Therefore, our ethical considerations for conservation treatment focused on the author's intent, and the context in which the books were written, printed, and sold. However, since Pokagon states that birch bark holds a spiritual significance to him, we took this into consideration in our studies and treatment plans. For example, we did not throw away any of the unused scraps of birch bark we collected for study and model-making, but instead returned them to the forest.

A major condition concern with birch bark is that it splits and delaminates over time. When evaluating the longevity of paper, conservators consider the amounts of stable and strong cellulose compared to other, more damaging components in the paper that are found in plants, such as lignin, which breaks down into acids and causes deterioration. Birch bark has a much lower percentage of cellulose than paper, and the permeable areas of lenticels make the bark even weaker.[52] As the bark ages it will become less flexible and split. This, coupled with the natural desiccation of the pectin between the laminates, leads to the natural delamination of the layers over time.[53] The peeling occurs between the two types of cork cells from different times in the tree's seasonal growth.[54] However, with proper handling and storage, deterioration can be slowed and largely prevented. Fortunately, birch bark is very resistant to deterioration through chemical reactions because it does not readily absorb water due to the waxes and oil found in the bark, and therefore has a low moisture content. It is not prone to acid hydrolysis, which requires water, and birch bark does not readily absorb water.[55]

FIGURE 22. Delamination of pages, *The Red Man's Greeting* (AC85 P7565 893r), Houghton Library, Harvard University.

The main condition issues for the books we assessed for treatment were splits in the bark and delamination of the layers (figure 22). This was caused both by the natural aging and deterioration of birch bark, and the way birch bark is strained in the oversewn bookbinding structures. Other condition problems we observed include accretions, bundles of disrupted fibers, planar distortions, and handling damage. The betulin residue on the surface of the pages is also easily disrupted, as can be observed where someone erased some graphite on the corner of a page in the *The Red Man's Rebuke*, making visible the darker orange layer below. Although mending tears, flattening distortions, and resewing books are common treatments for book conservators, we had to completely rethink our usual techniques to fit the challenges presented by the birch bark.[56]

Repairs to breaks and delamination required the use of carefully selected adhesives. We had to consider the matte, betulin-covered surface, with a risk that the surface quality can change during treatment. While conservators work with both water- and alcohol-based adhesives when making repairs, only water-based adhesives were considered for birch bark. Alcohols (a common component of conservation-sound adhesives) can extract components in birch bark and should therefore be avoided.[57] We also considered the composition of the adhesive in terms of its cultural appropriateness. Just as gelatin should not be used as an adhesive in the conservation of Buddhist artifacts due to the religion's spiritual belief in not killing animals, many Indigenous communities express a preference for natural, rather than synthetic, materials for the conservation treatment of organic Indigenous items.[58] Some synthetic materials degrade considerably slower than the organic materials they are used on, and will not solubilize for future removal, if needed. The use of biodegradable adhesives with organic items allows for the material to naturally decompose and return to the earth. For all these reasons, wheat starch paste and methyl cellulose were tested for treatment.[59] Although chemically synthesized, methyl cellulose was considered because it is made of cellulose (a component of birch bark), and it is water soluble, easily reversible, and breaks down naturally as it ages. The final choice was methyl cellulose because it is also more flexible and has weaker adhesion, a desirable quality in an adhesive used on delicate items because the repair is more likely to fail than causing further damage to the item. Also, wheat starch paste is known to contract as it dries, and because of the laminate structure of birch bark, the contraction of wheat starch paste was a concern because it could lead to the delamination of the layer to which the repair is adhered. When testing the flexibility of different repair materials on samples of birch bark, the repairs executed with methyl cellulose were considerably more flexible when compared to those executed with a very dilute wheat starch paste.

A "supported repair" is a mend that is completed using an adhesive applied to a support material to hold the damaged area together. The support material is often a narrow piece of thin, long-fibered tissue, which imparts strength but also allows it to remain very thin and unobtrusive. In the case of *The Red Man's Greeting* treated at Weissman Preservation Center, a machine-made 100 percent Japanese Kozo paper called NAJ Toned Tengucho was chosen for repairs.[60] The adhesive can be directly brushed onto the tissue, which is then adhered over the tear and placed under blotting paper and weight to dry. Another technique is to make a "remoistenable repair tissue," where the adhesive is applied and allowed to dry on the tissue, which can later be reactivated for use with a solvent, most often water or ethanol. Remoistenable tissue is often used when working with sensitive surfaces because it allows for the use of a very thin tissue, as well as a very controlled amount of adhesive and moisture. The use of remoistenable tissue also reduces the sheen of the adhesive, as methyl cellulose is quite shiny when it dries. Controlling the adhesive in this way allows for a more successful match to the matte surface of birch bark. Remoistenable tissue is also the sounder choice when moisture must be limited during mending. Although birch bark is resistant to water, pretreatment tests on samples showed that the betulin residue on the inner (darker) face of the bark darkens when saturated with water. This was mostly reversed with proper drying but should still be avoided. Using remoistenable tissue also allowed thinner repair tissues to be used for more transparent repairs.

When repairing a tear in paper, a conservator can often adhere the support material to only one side of the sheet. This is because paper is a network of intertwined fibers formed into a single sheet. Because birch bark is a laminar structure, a mend on one side of the sheet will only repair the tear on that one layer of bark; therefore, our technique for tear repair had to be adjusted. Mends were applied to both sides of the birch pages. Because most of the tears are at the edges of the pages, or at the punched sewing holes, the ends of the tissue mending strips were extended past the edge of the pages wrapping them around to the other side. This enveloped the tears and kept the edges from delaminating.

Rebinding

When looking at different copies of Pokagon's books, we observed many that are disbound and remain as loose pages. Often the ribbons disintegrated, leading to an unintentional disbinding, while sometimes people purposely remove the ribbons so they can read the text more easily. This is a good solution to prevent the flexing and splitting of the pages. However, we were concerned with leaving the pages loose because they may abrade and catch on each other, leading to further delamination and tears. This is a concern when researchers use the books, and the loose pages may get out of order when returned to their housings. A bound structure prevents this from happening. When possible, book conservators prefer books to remain bound because this allows users to handle the book in its original format and experience it as the maker intended, and it prevents dissociation and loss of material. When the rebinding of a book is required, book conservators are skilled at rethinking the original bookbinding structure whenever it was damaging the textblock. In the case of the oversewn *The Red Man's Greeting* and *The Red Man's Rebuke*, a new bookbinding structure was needed to reduce or eliminate the severe flexing of the page against the bound edge, because most of the splits in the pages are directly attributed to the original binding structure, which caused the page to flex up to 180 degrees when used. So, while it is preferable to maintain the original sewing structure as evidence of the book's history, exceptions are made in situations such as this, when the structure is causing damage and prevents safe use.

Several established techniques for rebinding loose pages were considered. One structure is a post-binding, which is made after encapsulating the pages in clear archival polyester sleeves (also referred to as Mylar or Melinex), and is a structure often used for rebinding damaged scrapbooks. However, this solution was found to be unsuitable for these books. Kaye specializes in the conservation of papyrus, another plant-based laminate substrate that has similar properties to birch bark. She advises against encapsulating a laminate material, as the static in polyester leads to delamination of layers, and when it comes to birch bark, the static also disturbs the betulin residue. Additionally, being able to handle birch bark is an incredibly tactile and unique experience, so encapsulating the pages prevents a full understanding and experience of the book. Another established rebinding option is attaching the loose pages together with thin strips of paper or tissue (what conservators refer to as "guarding") to create folios that then can be nested together and sewn. This is also not a good option for a laminate structure because the pages would have to be guarded on both sides to prevent delamination, which would cause too much strain and distortion on the bound edges, potentially leading to breakage where the guards are adhered and the pages flex.

Using birch bark she collected in the woods of Maine, Sjoblom made models of different book structures to test how they functioned and developed a safe and elegant solution. To prevent the flexing of the pages where they were damaged, the movement of the page was shifted to the edge of the page rather than the margin. The original sewing holes were used to secure the pages to stubs of Japanese paper. A stub is typically a narrow strip (often less than an inch) of paper sewn between sections of a book for the purpose of attaching loose plates, maps, etc., extending the margin and thus allowing free flexing.[61] In her model of a stubbed binding, Sjoblom found the paper stub flexed instead of the birch bark, preventing damage. The paper for the stubs is of medium-weight. This paper was selected because it has a flexible drape, allows the pages to lie flat when opened, and is strong enough that the weight of the page does not cause the stub to slump or become distorted. The pages were attached to the stubs in a manner that ensured that the sewing holes and fore edge of the textblock remained aligned. A hole punch tool was used to punch holes in

FIGURE 23. Completed treatment by Sjoblom for *The Red Man's Greeting* (AC85 P7565 893r), Weissman Preservation Center, Houghton Library, Harvard University.

the stubs, and then thin strips of lightweight tissue were passed through the holes to secure the stub and page together, acting as tackets. The tissue tackets were secured to themselves with wheat starch paste. To keep the page from flexing and moving away from the stub when the page is turned, small tabs of remoistenable tissue were also adhered along the spine edge of the page, securing it to the stub. The original green ribbon was replaced through only the first page of the book, suggesting the original structure, but not restricting the opening of the book. This new structure is reversible, meaning that it can be undone without damage to the birch bark pages. This was an important element of selecting a new bookbinding structure and allows for new ideas and future considerations (figure 23).

These images show the new stubbed bookbinding structure and ease of opening. In the lower right, the book is opened to the center, showing the sewing thread through the center of the folded section of the stubs. In the upper right image, the stub is visible on the verso of the left page. The tissue tackets pass between the original punched holes, and because the tissue is thin and a sympathetic color to the birch bark, it is not visually distracting.

Handling for Long-Term Preservation

Because the main condition concerns for birch bark are delamination and disrupted fibers, custodians and users of these books must avoid any rough surfaces. This includes the uncovered foam and padded wedges often found in reading rooms. If book cradles or wedges are required during use, placing a smooth piece of paper beneath the birch bark while it is in a support will prevent abrasion. Smooth surfaces will reduce friction and prevent anything from catching on the bark. Folders made of ten- or twenty-point cardstock can be used to store birchbark books or pages and help with transferring an item in and out of a larger box or moving it around a table. As with any thin and delicate item, it is good to use a stiff board to support the item when it is being lifted or moved. Because birch bark becomes stiffer and more brittle with age, flexing of the bark should be kept to a minimum. To turn pages, the use of tools is recommended, such as tabs of stiff paper that can be inserted between pages to turn them. Because the surface of birch bark is soft, matte, and can easily abrade or become marked and burnished, avoid using any sharp or hard items to turn pages. It is also very important to have clean and dry hands, because oils and dirt easily transfer and stain the bark.[62]

It is also important to note the misperceptions about wearing white gloves when handling library and archival materials. While gloves are appropriate for certain collection materials, such as photographic prints, negatives, slides, and many three-dimensional objects containing metals, it can be harmful to books, paper, and especially these thin birch bark pages. Gloves, which are often ill-fitting, lead to a lack of mobility and impaired tactile sensation.[63] Cotton gloves are very absorbent and are known to pick up dirt and debris from a user's surroundings, accumulating dirt on the outer surface of the gloves. When it comes to birch bark, they will harm the betulin residue, and will get caught on delaminated areas and disrupted fiber bundles. Studies on the effects of handling with clean, bare hands show no detrimental effects.[64] Simply requiring users to thoroughly wash their hands with soap and water before examining the books is an adequate requirement.

Copies of the books that are still bound will have reduced readability due to the oversewing and should be handled with extreme care. Opening the book too wide can stress the pages and cause splits. Depending on the use of the book, the availability of digitized images, and access guidelines for the institution or collection, disbinding may be considered. If the book is disbound, a protective enclosure is vital to prevent damage and dissociation of pages during storage. However, custodians of the books may choose to keep the books bound as an example of the original structure and history. In such a case, it is possible to provide a facsimile, images, and limit handling.

Exhibition Concerns

Testing completed at the Canadian Conservation Institute (CCI) revealed that different sources of light can cause damage to the inner cambium (darker side) of birch bark. Different colored birch bark samples were exposed to various light sources, including both natural and artificial light, and the color change was measured at different intervals of exposure. All light sources cause the darker bark to initially darken further, followed by fading. Partially UV-filtered daylight through a window causes the most change, leading to rapid darkening and then fading.[65] Therefore, exposure to light should be limited, especially daylight. As the testing at CCI was performed on the inner, darker face of the bark and showed that there is greater color change on this layer, it may be best to display pages printed on the lighter, outer face of the bark when exhibiting Pokagon's books.

When assessing the light sensitivity of materials on display, birch bark can be categorized as a dried plant material, which falls under the "most sensitive" category.[66] In this case, no single page of Pokagon's books should be displayed for more than three to four months, and lighting should be kept low, ideally at five footcandles (50 lux) or less of illumination. If one display page can be replaced with another in the same book, then the pages can usually be turned to prolong the time a single book is on exhibit. However, due to the strain on the pages, we do not recommend the books be displayed open when they are still bound in the original structure. The materials in direct contact with the books on display should be chemically stable. It is useful to place a barrier between the book and the exhibit case floor or wall.[67] Of course, reaching out to exhibit preparators or conservators for advice on how to properly display such delicate materials is always encouraged.[68]

Storage

When it comes to the sensitive surface of birch bark, it is important to prevent friction between adjacent leaves in storage, especially when the leaves are loose and no longer bound. This can be accomplished using smooth interleaving papers, available through most archival supply vendors. Most importantly, the books should be placed in custom protective enclosures when not in use, which protects them from dust, light, and mechanical damage. The books should be housed in enclosures that prevent flexing and abrasion. Drop-spine boxes and phase boxes are available through a wide variety of vendors and library binders but are better suited for larger books. The small size of the Pokagon books makes it difficult to create sturdy enclosures for them, but they can be placed in a custom enclosure within a larger box. Wrappers made of folder- or cardstock provide support and protection for small books and are more easily constructed in-house with minimal equipment.[69] Sjoblom created a four-flap wrapper for Harvard's *The Red Man's Greeting*, made of ten-point folder stock, providing a smooth surface on which the book can also be handled. The four-flap wrapper was placed in a prefabricated hardcover folder for additional support. Pieces of Volara foam were used to pad out the folder to fit the book in its four-flap housing. Handling instructions and a picture of the original binding structure were printed out and adhered inside the binder.

Small books can also be stored in acid-free, lignin-free, buffered folders, with optional wrappers or buffered paper to protect from abrasion.[70] Folders can then be housed in chemically stable document storage boxes. Document storage boxes come in both flat and upright varieties, and either may work for the Pokagon books. In upright boxes, folders should be well supported to prevent slumping, so spacers can be made from chemically stable materials (and often can be purchased with the boxes) to fill empty space to support the folders.[71] Overfilling a box will crush the books. Envelopes are sometimes used to house small books but do not provide adequate support, and damage often occurs when repeatedly pulling the books in and out. String, rubber bands, and tape should never be used to hold the books together if they are falling apart. If needed, the books can be carefully wrapped in a soft, lignin-free tissue paper and placed in a larger protective enclosure.

Proper environmental conditions will also prevent damage to birch bark. Environmental factors to consider include temperature, relative humidity (RH), light, pollution, and pests. Birch bark is very resistant to water compared to paper. Whereas paper will often absorb water in a few seconds, birch bark requires twenty-four hours for at least partial absorption.[72] However, early and late cells in the bark respond differently to changes in RH, which can lead to curling of the bark.[73] Because the desiccation of the natural pectin adhesive between the layers leads to delamination, a low RH is not recommended. Kicknosway also takes this into account, as he is at a high elevation in Montana, and notices the difference in how dry the bark gets compared to when he works with birch bark on the East Coast. The cracking and curling of birch bark happen faster and easier when the RH is very low. Birch bark can therefore be safely stored at about 55 percent RH.[74] Anything higher introduces the risk of mold growth for typical library collection materials such as paper, leather, and parchment. This is not as much of a concern for birch bark because of its resistance to biodeterioration, but since birch bark books are often stored with other paper-based collections, this is a suitable RH. When it comes to an ideal temperature for the storage of organic materials, 65–70 degrees Fahrenheit is the accepted standard.[75]

As discussed earlier, exposure to light can cause color change and should be limited by storing the books in protective enclosures. Color change can occur even in dark temperature- and humidity-controlled environments, and elevated and fluctuating conditions can also cause color change, especially in the red to orange-red colored winter barks.[76] Although very difficult to control in most building environments, gaseous contaminants such as sulfur dioxide, nitrogen dioxide, and ozone, as well as various particulates, are also found in libraries and archives.[77] A proper heating, ventilation, and air conditioning (HVAC) system is a worthy investment for ensuring the longevity of Pokagon's books, as well as library and archival collections at large. Fortunately, birch bark is very resistant to fungal and insect damage, largely due to the betulin content. If the storage areas are kept clean and the environmental controls remain steady, concerns about pests can be kept to a minimum.

Conclusions

As conservators of library and archival collections, it is important for us to understand the chemistry and working properties of the materials people use to create books, but it is also important for us to understand why they use them. This is not always easy, and with a person as complex and full of contradictions as Pokagon, many questions remain unanswered. One of the biggest questions we cannot answer is who the person or group was who provided the birch bark for Pokagon's works. Our conversations with current artists working with birch bark did, however, help us better understand the technical aspects of its harvesting, processing, and range of use. More than that, they showed us the underlying messages conveyed by birch bark, and their deep meaning to the Neshnabé culture, with its strong artistic traditions and craftsmanship. We see this in Church's basketry, which speaks to the loss of black ash and the resulting gap in generational knowledge that goes into basket weaving. We see this in Kicknosway's work on YouTube and Instagram, which thousands of people follow to learn about his traditional Ojibwe quillwork techniques. The use of a live material, such as birch bark, honors its meaning and tradition through millennia. Kicknosway perfectly summarized the importance of the use of a live material when he said:

> I personally cannot use [bark from a dead tree] for this style . . . it has to be a live tree. And to me, it means so much more, right? It's like to some it may be, oh you're harming the tree. . . . But to me it's like the cultural aspect of keeping something so rare alive, by using something that's alive. It just means so much more to me. . . . It's like we use so much of it, and knowing that it's alive, and that I'm keeping something alive. This art's alive—it just hits me on a whole different level.

The use of birch bark in Pokagon's books has been described partially as a marketing technique to attract buyers in the Victorian tourist trade.[78] However, through our research and artist interviews, we understand the use of birch bark as a strong political and environmental statement by Pokagon, which carries with it a unique charm that draws people in more readily to learn from his writings. The knowledge and tradition involved in the use of birch bark should be in the forefront for all who handle the books. Likewise, we must consider Pokagon's strong tie to the land, further emphasized by his use of Potawatomi place names in these texts to remind the reader of the historical and current presence of the Potawatomi. Pokagon's use of birch bark not only brings up questions about how the Neshnabé historically and currently use birch bark for utilitarian and artistic purposes, but also brings up questions about the influence of treaties, land use, and sovereignty as they relate to access to birch forests through the centuries, to the present day. When studying Pokagon's books, we must consider who made them, where the birch bark came from, and why the birch bark was chosen. We still do not have answers to all these questions but gaining a deeper understanding of birch bark as a material and its use in Neshnabé culture helped us perform thoughtful treatments of these books, allowing future researchers to study them firsthand and continue seeking greater knowledge and understanding of a material and its role in Neshnabé futurism.

Notes

1. We are including both *The Red Man's Rebuke* and *The Red Man's Greeting* in our count.
2. Cathleen A. Baker, *From the Hand to the Machine: Nineteenth-Century American Paper and Mediums: Technologies, Materials, and Conservation* (Ann Arbor, MI: Legacy Press), 1.
3. Kenneth L. Quigley and Harold M. Babcock, "Birch Timber Resources of North America," Birch Symposium (Durham, NH, 1969), *Birch Symposium Proceedings*, US Forest Service, https://www.srs.fs.usda.gov/pubs/48010, 6.
4. W. Keith Moser, Mark H. Hansen, Dale Gormanson, Jonathan Gilbert, Alexandra Wrobel, Marla R. Emery, and Michael J. Dockry, "Paper Birch (Wiigwaas) of the Lake States, 1980–2010. With Special Emphasis on Bark Characteristics in the Territories Ceded in the Treaties of 1836, 1837, 1842, and 1854," United States Department of Agriculture, Forest Service, Northern Research Station, General Technical Report NRS-149, April 2015, 1.
5. Lawrence O. Safford, John C. Bjorkbom, and John C. Zasada, "Betula Papyrifera Marsh: Paper Birch; Betulaceae—Birch Family," *Silvics of North America*, vol. 2, *Hardwoods* (Washington, DC: United States Government Printing Office, 1990), 1 and 7.
6. Kelly Church, email message to the authors, April 19, 2022.
7. Kelly Church, email message to the authors, April 19, 2022.
8. Safford, Bjorkbom, and Zasada, "Betula Papyrifera Marsh," 1.
9. Steve Garske, "Characteristics of Sites Supporting Large Paper Birch in the 1836, 1837 and 1842 Ceded Territories," Great Lakes Indian Fish & Wildlife Commission, Project Report 17-06, May 2017, 2.
10. Crystal Maitland, "Learning to Conserve a Kashmiri Birch Bark Manuscript," *Book and Paper Group Annual* 35 (2016): 49–60, 51.
11. Maitland, "Learning to Conserve a Kashmiri Birch Bark Manuscript," 51.
12. Season Tse, Carole Dignard, Sonia Kata, and Eric J. Henderson, "A Study of the Light Sensitivity of Birch Bark," *Studies in Conservation* 63, no. 7 (2018): 423–40, 423.
13. Holly H. Krueger, "Conservation of the Library of Congress' Gandhara Scroll: A Collaborative Process," *Book and Paper Group Annual* 29 (2008): 29–34, 30.
14. Simon Pokagon, "Indian Native Skill," *The Chautauquan* 26 (1898): 540–42, 540.
15. Marla R. Emery, Alexandra Wrobel, Mark H. Hansen, Michael Dockry, W. Keith Moser, Kekek Jason Stark, and Jonathan H. Gilbert, "Using Traditional Ecological Knowledge as a Basis for Targeted Forest Inventories: Paper Birch (Betula Papyrifera) in the US Great Lakes Region," *Journal of Forestry* 112, no. 2 (2014): 207–14, 208. "Cultural keystone species are culturally salient species that shape in a major way the cultural identity of a people. Their importance is reflected in the fundamental roles these species play in diet, materials, medicine, and/or spiritual practices." Ann Garibaldi and Nancy Turner, "Cultural Keystone Species: Implications for Ecological Conservation and Restoration," *Ecology and Society* 9, no. 3 (2004): 1, appendix 1.
16. Emery et al., "Using Traditional Ecological Knowledge," 207–14.

17. Simon Pokagon, *The Red Man's Rebuke* (Hartford, MI: C. H. Engle, 1893) and *The Red Man's Greeting* (Hartford, MI: C. H. Engle, 1893), "By the Author."
18. Kelly Church, Woodland Arts, 2021, https://www.woodlandarts.com.
19. Wisecup includes an image of some of these items in her figure of Indian splint work from Pokagon, *Queen of the Woods.*
20. Great Lakes Fish and Wildlife Commission, *Treaty Rights Recognition and Affirmation,* https://glifwc.org/Recognition_Affirmation/.
21. Detailed information on the Pokagon Band's history can be found on their website: Pokagon Band of Potawatomi, "History," 2021, https://www.pokagonband-nsn.gov/our-culture/history.
22. "The number of birch trees on timberland in the ceded territories [in the Great Lakes region] has decreased since 1980, going from 611 million trees ≥5 inches to 298 million, a 49-percent decrease." Moser et al., "Paper Birch (Wiigwaas) of the Lake States," 7.
23. Kelly Church, email message to the authors, September 10, 2021.
24. Pokagon, *The Red Man's Rebuke* and *The Red Man's Greeting,* "By the Author."
25. Shannon Croft and Rolf Mathewes, "Barking up the Right Tree: Understanding Birch Bark Artifacts from the Canadian Plateau, British Columbia," *BC Studies* 180 (January 2014): 83–122, 91.
26. Kelly Church, email message to the authors, September 10, 2021.
27. Emery et al., "Using Traditional Ecological Knowledge," 208; Devan Kicknosway, *How I Harvest Birch Bark*, YouTube, August 24, 2020, https://www.youtube.com/watch?v=iQDPWSCQs7g.
28. Keewaydinoquay also published under her English name, Margaret Peschel (1919–99).
29. This is illustrated in images in Karen C. Danielsen and Stephen White Jr., "Characteristics of Wiigwaasi-Mitig (Paper Birch, Betula Papyri/Em Marsh)," *USDA Forest Service Agreement #0 1·JY·11 23 1300-0AS*, Great Lakes Indian Fish & Wildlife Commission, 2003, 6–11.
30. Wendy M. Geniusz, *Our Knowledge Is Not Primitive: Decolonizing Botanical Anishinaabe Teachings* (Syracuse, NY: Syracuse University Press, 2009), 183.
31. Kicknosway, *How I Harvest Birch Bark.*
32. Skye Haggerty, "Barking Up the Right Tree (Part 1)," *Royal Alberta Museum Blog*, July 3, 2019, https://royalalbertamuseumblog.tumblr.com/post/186034667173/barking-up-the-right-tree-part-1; Kelly Church, email message to the authors, September 10, 2021; Devan Kicknosway in discussion with the authors, August 31, 2021.
33. Kelly Church, email message to the authors, September 10, 2021.
34. In personal communication with Kelly Church, she notes that artist Pat Bruderer (Halfmoon Woman; Peter Ballantyne Cree Nation) uses winter bark for birch bark bitings. (See Emily Reily, "Indigenous Artists Keep Birch Bark Biting Alive," *Washington Post*, August 31, 2021).
35. Pokagon's birch bark books examined in person by Sjoblom or Kaye: *The Red Man's Greeting* (1893), Houghton Library, Harvard; *The Red Man's Rebuke* (1893), *Pottawatomie Book of Genesis* (1901), and *Algonquin Legends of Paw Paw Lake* (1899) at the University of Michigan, Special Collections Research Center; *The Red Man's Rebuke* (1893) at The Bentley Historical Library, University of Michigan. Examined digital copies: *The Red Man's Rebuke* (1893), Smithsonian Libraries; *The Red Man's Greeting* (1893), Florida International University; *The Red Man's Greeting* (1893) and *Pottawatomie Book of Genesis*

(1901), Newberry Library, Chicago; *Algonquin Legends of Paw Paw Lake* (1899) and *Algonquin Legends of South Haven* (1900), Pokagon Band Archives: Wiwkwébthëgen.

36. Jonathan Berliner, "Written in the Birch Bark: The Linguistic-Material Worldmaking of Simon Pokagon," *PMLA* 125, no. 1 (January 2010): 73–91, 87–88.
37. Berliner, "Written in the Birch Bark," 87–88.
38. Topash-Caldwell, "The Birch-Bark Booklets of Simon Pokagon," *Michigan History* (July/August 2018): 50–54, 53.
39. Berliner, "Written in the Birch Bark," 82.
40. See the title images for chapter *The Red Man's Greeting/Rebuke* in this volume.
41. See title images for chapters *Pottawattamie Book of Genesis, Algonquin Legends of Paw Paw Lake, Algonquin Legends of South Haven.*
42. For a detailed discussion and examples of birch bark books from this region, refer to Daisy Todd's blog post for the British Library: "Everything You Need to Know about Birch Bark Book Conservation," *British Library Collection Care Blog*, August 10, 2017, https://blogs.bl.uk/collectioncare/2017/08/from-sawdust-to-gold-dust-the-conservation-of-a-c16th-birch-bark-book.html.
43. The catalog entry and more images can be found here: Pokagon Band of Potawatomi, "Wiwkwébthëgen," https://www.wiwkwebthegen.com/digital-heritage/quilled-birch-bark-book.
44. See Wisecup's chapter for an image and more information on this book.
45. Daniel Radus, "Margaret Boyd's Quillwork History," *Early American Literature* 53, no. 2 (2018): 513–37.
46. Kacie Amann, "Birch Bark Poems," *Rauner Special Collections Library Blog*, July 8, 2016, https://raunerlibrary.blogspot.com/2016/07/birch-bark-poems.html.
47. An image of *Bayview the Beautiful* can be found in Wisecup's chapter.
48. Donald Saff and Deli Sacilotto, *History and Processes of Printmaking* (New York: Holt, Rinehart, and Winston, 1978), 7.
49. See figure 19 for an example of the crooked printing on some pages.
50. Pokagon, *The Red Man's Rebuke*, 1.
51. Resources we used to learn about conservation and working with Indigenous collections include Native American Graves Protection Act (NAGPRA), https://www.nps.gov/subjects/nagpra/index.htm; Association of Tribal Archives, Libraries, and Museums (ATALM), https://atalm.org/; Indian Arts Research Center at the School for Advanced Research (SAR), Guidelines for Collaboration, https://guidelinesforcollaboration.info/; and Protocols for Native American Archival Materials, https://www2.nau.edu/libnap-p/index.html.
52. Maitland, "Learning to Conserve a Kashmiri Birch Bark Manuscript," 52.
53. Krueger, "Conservation of the Library of Congress' Gandhara Scroll," 30.
54. Tse, Dignard, Kata, and Henderson,"A Study of the Light Sensitivity of Birch Bark," 423.
55. D. G. Suryawanshi, "Like Paper: Birch Bark and Its Chemical Composition," *Restaurator* 27, no. 2 (2006): 103–13, 111.
56. For images and more information on the conservation treatment of the books, please see the paper by Sjoblom and Kaye, "Conservation and Study of Simon Pokagon's Birch Bark Books," in the American Institute of Conservation's *Book and Paper Group Annual*, vol. 41 (2022).
57. Maitland, "Learning to Conserve a Kashmiri Birch Bark Manuscript," 56.

58. Miriam Clavir discusses First Nations perspectives on preservation in detail in her book *Preserving What Is Valued: Museums, Conservation, and First Nations* (Vancouver: UBC Press, 2002); her research focused on interviews about conservation and preservation with First Nations communities primarily in British Columbia. Individual communities have different guidelines and opinions of care and treatment of items originating from their communities. This generalization about treatment preference was taken as a starting point in considering perspectives and questions about treatment, and communication with stakeholder communities is vital.

59. Methyl cellulose (MC) is a cellulose ether with a methyl functional group substitution. It is a fibrous, soft white powder that is used as a substitute for natural gums. It forms a highly viscous colloidal solution in cold water that reversibly gels when heated. Methyl cellulose dries to a clear film with very little shrinkage (*CAMEO Materials Database*, Museum of Fine Arts, Boston, https://cameo.mfa.org/wiki/Main_Page). Wheat starch consists of polysaccharide granules that compose about 70 percent of wheat flour. Wheat starch is separated from gluten and fibrous particles by sieving followed by wash flotation. It is composed of 18 to 27 percent amylose. When heated with water, wheat starch forms a low viscosity solution that does not change with heating time. It thickens substantially on cooling to form an opaque gel. Wheat starch dries to form a strong bond. Wheat starch paste is the primary adhesive used by paper conservators for hinging, mending, lining, and reinforcement (CAMEO Materials Database; AIC Book and Paper Catalog).

60. The paper is made by Hidaka Washi in Kochi, Japan, and purchased from Hiromi Paper, Inc. in 5.0 and 7.3 g/m² weights.

61. Don Etherington and Matt T. Roberts, *Bookbinding and the Conservation of Books: A Dictionary of Descriptive Terminology* (Washington, DC: Library of Congress, 1982), 253.

62. For more detailed information on handling books, and links to handling videos, look at University of Michigan, "U-M Library: Handling and Supporting Books," 2020, https://tinyurl.com/4rpxnmxh.

63. Cathleen A. Baker and Randy Silverman, "Misperceptions about White Gloves," *International Preservation News* 37 (December 2005): 4–9, 4.

64. Baker and Silverman, "Misperceptions about White Gloves," 5.

65. Tse, Dignard, Kata, and Henderson, "A Study of the Light Sensitivity of Birch Bark," 438.

66. See "U-M Exhibit Guidelines," https://tinyurl.com/yckmj7vh.

67. For detailed information on the proper exhibition of library and archival materials, refer to ANSI/NISO Standards Z39.79-2001, *Environmental Conditions for Exhibiting Library and Archival Materials: An American National Standard*. Bethesda, MD: NISO Press, 2001.

68. The American Institute for Conservation provides a tool for finding professionals on their website, https://www.culturalherit, age.org/about-conservation/find-a-conservator.

69. Northeast Document Conservation Center, "Preservation Leaflet 4.1: Storage and Handling for Books and Artifacts on Paper," 2012, https://www.nedcc.org/assets/media/documents/Preservation%20Leaflets/4.1_StorageHandling_Print.pdf, 2.

70. Northeast Document Conservation Center, "Preservation Leaflet 4.1," 4.

71. Northeast Document Conservation Center, "Preservation Leaflet 4.1," 5.

72. Suryawanshi, "Like Paper," 105.

73. Maitland, "Learning to Conserve a Kashmiri Birch Bark Manuscript," 52.

74. William K. Wilson, *Environmental Guidelines for the Storage of Paper Records*, Technical

Report NISO-TR01-1995 (Bethesda, MA: NISO Press, 1995), http://www.niso.org/sites/default/files/2017-08/tr01.pdf, 1.

75. Wilson, *Environmental Guidelines for the Storage of Paper Records*, 2.
76. Tse, Dignard, Kata, and Henderson, "A Study of the Light Sensitivity of Birch Bark," 439.
77. Wilson, *Environmental Guidelines for the Storage of Paper Records*, 2.
78. Berliner, "Written in the Birch Bark," 80.

Acknowledgments

Blaire Morseau is humbled and grateful to all the contributors of this volume. By sharing their expertise and insights, they have breathed new life into Simon Pokagon's birch bark stories. She thanks Marcus Winchester and Jason S. Wesaw for being the first to share these incredible birch bark books with her in the summer of 2017, just shortly after the Pokagon Band officially acquired the collection in their archives. An amplified thank-you goes to Bmejwen Kyle Malott for his tireless translation of the Potawatomi language throughout the collection. She'd also like to thank Michigan State University's former editor in chief, Julie Loehr, for encouraging this project when Blaire met her at the Michigan Historical Society's annual conference back in 2018. All royalties from the sales of this text will be donated to the Pokagon Band of Potawatomi Archives program.

Kelly Wisecup thanks Blaire Morseau for feedback and conversations about Pokagon throughout my research. I'm also indebted to conversations with Blaire, Paul Erickson, Marieka Kaye, Fritz Swanson, and Oa Sjoblom about Pokagon and nineteenth-century printing. Thanks to Katy Chiles for asking the question that led to this research; to Michael Kelly for conversations about bibliography; to students Rivers Leche, Nia Robles Del Pino, and Isabel St. Arnold for feedback on an early draft; and to Kyle Mallott for discussing Pokagon's granddaughters. I'm also grateful to the students in English 374, Fall 2019, for conversations about *The Red Man's Greeting*, and to the Fall 2021 Newberry fellows' seminar for transformative feedback.

This research would not have been possible without the many experts who shared their time and knowledge with us. Oa Sjoblom and Marieka Kaye are particularly thankful to Dr. Morseau and Dr. Wisecup for including us in conversations about these books, which deepened our understanding immensely. Thank you to Marcus Winchester, former director of the Pokagon Band Center for History and Culture. We are so honored that artists Kelly Church and Devan Kicknosway agreed to discuss how they harvest and use birch bark and answered our many questions about the material as it relates to Pokagon's books. Thanks goes to Ben Secunda, NAGPRA project manager for the University of Michigan, for input on NAGPRA guidelines. These conversations exponentially added to our understanding of the characteristics of birch bark and the book production.

Oa is grateful for the many conservators she spoke to: Katherine Beaty, Laura Larkin, Yasmeen Khan, Crystal Maitland, Daisy Todd, Liz Randell, Judy Jungle, T. Rose Holdcraft, and Erin Murphy, as well as Leslie Morris, curator of the collection at Houghton Library, Harvard University Native American Program, Native American Indigenous Student Working Group, and Meredith Vasta at the Harvard Peabody Museum. She is also grateful to the staff at Weissman Preservation Center for their support, ideas, and encouragement.

Marieka thanks the staff, curators, and librarians at the University of Michigan Library's Special Collections Research Center, the Bentley Historical Library, and the William L. Clements Library for assisting with her viewing of their birch bark holdings. She is grateful for the direction and rich resources provided by Michael Kelly and Dr. Kiara Vigil at Amherst College during their Indigenous Book History course for the Rare Book School. Finally, thanks go to Shannon Zachary, head of preservation and conservation at U-M, for supporting her research endeavors.

Contributors

Corinne Kasper is an enrolled member of the Pokagon Band of Potawatomi Indians and a PhD student in linguistics at the University of Chicago. While in the academy, she focuses on second-language and heritage-language Potawatomi morphosyntax, pragmatics, and discourse. In a better world, she has been learning the language since either twelve or fifteen, who's to say. She is Turtle Clan and deeply indebted to all her Potawatomi teachers and mentors.

Marieka Kaye (she/her/hers) manages the conservation lab at the University of Michigan Library. Marieka started working in the field of library preservation in 1998, during her senior year at Brandeis University. She received an MA and Certificate of Advanced Study in art conservation from SUNY Buffalo State in 2006 and a Master of Library and Information Science from San Jose State University in 2011. Prior to starting her position at U-M in 2013, she served as a conservator at The Huntington Library in San Marino, California, for eight years.

Bmejwen Kyle Malott is a speaker and teacher of Bodwéwadmimwen (Potawatomi language). He is an enrolled citizen of the Pokagon Band of Potawatomi Indians to which he is a direct descendant of Chief Leopold Pokagon and is of the Eagle Clan. Bmejwen was taught by fluent speakers of the Forest County Potawatomi and has spent over ten years working in and studying Potawatomi language and history.

Nicholas Marcelletti is a licensed professional geologist. He received his Bachelor of Science in geology from Hope College, Holland, Michigan, and Master of Science in geology from Eastern Kentucky University, Richmond, Kentucky. He has practiced geology for over twenty years. He has taught earth science at Macomb Community College since 2011, and from 2013 to 2018 he taught introduction to geology at Schoolcraft College. He plans on finding proof of Simon Pokagon's flood.

Blaire Morseau is Bear Clan and an enrolled citizen of the Pokagon Band of Potawatomi Indians. She is assistant professor of anthropology at the University of Massachusetts Boston and interim director of Native American and Indigenous Studies. Prior to her appointment at UMass Boston, she was the Pokagon Band's first full-time archivist and she launched the tribe's archives and dictionary website, Wiwkwébthëgen, to increase access and share knowledge with, by, and for Native peoples of the Great Lakes region.

Oa Sjoblom (she/her/hers) started working in conservation in 2010 in New Orleans. She received an MA in art conservation from SUNY Buffalo State in 2020, specializing in library and archive conservation. She was a Cathleen A. Baker Fellow at the University of Michigan Library conservation lab, and a graduate intern and then contractor at the Weissman Preservation Center at Harvard Library. She is currently a contract book conservator at the Historic Architecture, Conservation and Engineering Center of the National Park Service in Lowell, Massachusetts.

Kelly Wisecup is professor of English at Northwestern University, where she is also affiliated with the Center for Native American and Indigenous Research. She is author, most recently, of *Assembled for Use: Indigenous Compilation and the Archives of Early Native American Literatures* (2021) and coeditor, with Lisa Brooks, of *Plymouth Colony: Narratives of English Settlement and Native Resistance from the Mayflower to King Philip's War* (2022).

AMERICAN INDIAN STUDIES SERIES

Aazheyaadizi: Worldview, Language, and the Logics of Decolonization, Mark D. Freeland | 978-1-61186-380-2

As Sacred to Us: Simon Pokagon's Birch Bark Stories in Their Contexts, edited by Blaire Morseau | 978-1-61186-462-5

Bawaajimo: A Dialect of Dreams in Anishinaabe Language and Literature, Margaret Noodin | 978-1-61186-105-1

Centering Anishinaabeg Studies: Understanding the World through Stories, edited by Jill Doerfler, Niigaanwewidam James Sinclair, and Heidi Kiiwetinepinesiik Stark | 978-1-61186-067-2

Curator of Ephemera at the New Museum for Archaic Media, Heid E. Erdrich | 978-1-61186-246-1

Document of Expectations, Devon Abbott Mihesuah | 978-1-61186-011-5

Dragonfly Dance, Denise K. Lajimodiere | 978-0-87013-982-6

Encountering the Sovereign Other: Indigenous Science Fiction, Miriam C. Brown Spiers | 978-1-61186-405-2

Facing the Future: The Indian Child Welfare Act at 30, edited by Matthew L. M. Fletcher, Wenona T. Singel, and Kathryn E. Fort | 978-0-87013-860-7

Famine Pots: The Choctaw–Irish Gift Exchange, 1847–Present, edited by LeAnne Howe and Padraig Kirwan | 978-1-61186-369-7

Follow the Blackbirds, Gwen Nell Westerman | 978-1-61186-092-4

Gambling on Authenticity: Gaming, the Noble Savage, and the Not-So-New Indian, edited by Becca Gercken and Julie Pelletier | 978-1-61186-256-0

Indian Country: Telling a Story in a Digital Age, Victoria L. LaPoe and Benjamin Rex LaPoe II | 978-1-61186-226-3

The Indian Who Bombed Berlin and Other Stories, Ralph Salisbury | 978-0-87013-847-8

Indigenizing Philosophy through the Land: A Trickster Methodology for Decolonizing Environmental Ethics and Indigenous Futures, Brian Burkhart | 978-1-61186-330-7

Louise Erdrich's Justice Trilogy: Cultural and Critical Contexts, edited by Connie A. Jacobs and Nancy J. Peterson | 978-1-61186-403-8

Masculindians: Conversations about Indigenous Manhood, edited by Sam McKegney| 978-1-61186-129-7

Mediating Indianness, edited by Cathy Covell Waegner | 978-1-61186-151-8

The Murder of Joe White: Ojibwe Leadership and Colonialism in Wisconsin, Erik M. Redix | 978-1-61186-145-7

National Monuments, Heid E. Erdrich | 978-0-87013-848-5

Ogimawkwe Mitigwaki (Queen of the Woods), Simon Pokagon | 978-0-87013-987-1

Ottawa Stories from the Springs: Anishinaabe dibaadjimowinan wodi gaa binjibaamigak wodi mookodjiwong e zhinikaadek, translated and edited by Howard Webkamigad | 978-1-61186-137-2

Picturing Worlds: Visuality and Visual Sovereignty in Contemporary Anishinaabe Literature, David Stirrup | 978-1-61186-352-9

Plain of Jars and Other Stories, Geary Hobson | 978-0-87013-998-7

Sacred Wilderness, Susan Power | 978-1-61186-111-2

Seeing Red—Hollywood's Pixeled Skins: American Indians and Film, edited by LeAnne Howe, Harvey Markowitz, and Denise K. Cummings | 978-1-61186-081-8

Self-Determined Stories: The Indigenous Reinvention of Young Adult Literature, Mandy Suhr-Sytsma | 978-1-61186-298-0

Shedding Skins: Four Sioux Poets, edited by Adrian C. Louis | 978-0-87013-823-2

Sounding Thunder: The Stories of Francis Pegahmagabow, Brian D. McInnes | 978-1-61186-225-6

Stories for a Lost Child, Carter Meland | 978-1-61186-244-7

Stories through Theories/Theories through Stories: North American Indian Writing, Storytelling, and Critique, edited by Gordon D. Henry Jr., Nieves Pascual Soler, and Silvia Martinez-Falquina | 978-0-87013-841-6

That Guy Wolf Dancing, Elizabeth Cook-Lynn | 978-1-61186-138-9

Those Who Belong: Identity, Family, Blood, and Citizenship among the White Earth Anishinaabeg, Jill Doerfler | 978-1-61186-169-3

Visualities: Perspectives on Contemporary American Indian Film and Art, edited by Denise K. Cummings | 978-0-87013-999-4

Visualities 2: More Perspectives on Contemporary American Indian Film and Art, edited by Denise K. Cummings | 978-1-61186-319-2

Writing Home: Indigenous Narratives of Resistance, Michael D. Wilson | 978-0-87013-818-8